In our lifetime, there are always people, events, trainings or books that shape who we are today and who we become tomorrow.

Art Horn is the founder and president of HORN, a highly regarded training organization that we have hired based on your votes, to deliver our 2-hour sales training session at the 2010 Partner Symposium.

This book will make all of us explore a truth that outstanding leaders possess so well: influential leadership starts within. It will further our abilities as leaders to align and inspire others.

We hope you'll enjoy reading *Beyond Ego*. We thought it would make an interesting token of our appreciation for your partnership in 2009.

Bell

The Bell Canada External Sales Channel

BEYOND EGO

Also by Art Horn

Skills for Sales Success
Gift of Leadership
Face It

BEYOND EGO

Influential Leadership Starts Within

ART HORN

Foreword by
ROBERT H. PITFIELD

ECW PRESS

Published by ECW Press
2120 Queen Street East, Suite 200, Toronto, Ontario, Canada M4E 1E2

LIBRARY AND ARCHIVES CANADA CATALOGUING IN PUBLICATION

Horn, Arthur H.
Beyond ego : influential leadership starts within / Art Horn.

ISBN 978-1-55022-774-1

1. Leadership. 2. Egoism. 3. Executive ability. 1. Title.

HD57.7.H665 2008   658.4'094   C2007-907084-1

Text and Cover Design: Tania Craan
Cover Image: Betsie Van der Meer
Typesetting: Mary Bowness
Production: Rachel Brooks
Printing: Thomson-Shore

The publication of *Beyond Ego* has been generously supported
by the Government of Canada through the Book Publishing
Industry Development Program (BPIDP).

Canada

DISTRIBUTION
CANADA: Jaguar Book Group, 100 Armstrong Ave., Georgetown, ON L7G 5S4
UNITED STATES: Independent Publishers Group, 814 North Franklin Street,
Chicago, IL 60610

PRINTED AND BOUND IN THE UNITED STATES

ECW PRESS
ecwpress.com

To Joan, my soulmate

CONTENTS

FOREWORD ix

PREFACE xi

PART III ■ MASTERY

FOREWORD

The first time I met Art was when he was leading a three-day coaching session for our senior team.

Our Domestic Division had for many years employed coaching as an essential part of driving our sales and service disciplines, which had earned them top marks for service and outstanding sales growth year over year. At the time of Art's session, we in the International Division had started to roll out coaching right through our organization, all the way down to our Personal Banking Officers in our branches. At the strong urging of one of our senior management team members, Pat Minicucci, we had agreed that if it was good enough for them, it should be good enough for us. Also, we had to admit—what did we know about coaching and egoless leadership anyway?

Well, after three days in that coaching session, we knew a whole lot more! We also knew that coaching, egoless leadership, judging but not being judgmental, listening and being wholly heard were things we simply had to learn to do.

At one point in the session, I was asked to sit in the middle of a circle of chairs, surrounded by International's senior management team. Art sat opposite me. He was to coach and I was to respond as openly and naturally as I felt I could. Art began to ask me questions about what I was working on, what I hoped to accomplish, what issues and concerns I had. And so the conversation went.

I can't tell you how long it lasted. I can tell you I will never forget it. I don't know if you have ever experienced someone listening to you deeply and without reservation. That's what Art did with me. He listened. He judged my answers but did not judge me. I felt that he cared about what I was doing and that he would help me in any way he could. I trusted him completely. If I could do something better, he would tell me, but not to show that he was smarter than I or knew all the answers. It was just because it would help me, period — with no regard to his own personal advantage or agenda.

As I read this book, coming upon familiar ideas and insights like old friends, I was brought back to our session with Art. The book reminds me of the challenge of personal change. For example, doing the session was harder than we thought it would be — we had to live it. We had to deal with those things we didn't know and weren't good at. Instituting coaching into our organization so that it is in our DNA, a fundamental part of who we are, has been harder still.

It is a journey we are committed to. We are already a good bank with as wonderfully diverse, talented, and dedicated a group of people as you could ever hope to stand shoulder to shoulder with. This journey is making us better: better leaders and better people.

So to Art, we give you and all your people who are helping us a big, big thanks and a gran abrazo! For you the reader, I hope you enjoy this book and ponder its thoughts. They are worth the chew. If you would like it to, *Beyond Ego* can start you on a road less traveled and one I believe you will be glad you took.

Robert H. Pitfield
Executive Vice-President
International Banking
Scotiabank

PREFACE

My hope is that you will get great value from this book. I wrote it with you in mind. Of course, I don't know you; I can only be confident that a certain curiosity has taken you this far, and I respect that curiosity.

The inspiration for the book came from people all around the world who have responded so favorably to its ideology. Had my colleagues and I not been received with such eye-opening gratitude, my fingers would never have danced — let alone danced so eagerly — across my keyboard.

Beyond Ego is not from one man alone with an inspired, singular insight. It could not have been written without the help of family, friends, colleagues, clients, and a reasonable amount of what I think is healthy personal angst. I am very grateful.

Let me thank, first and foremost, the contribution of my wife, Joan Berman, who over the last twenty years, in the most loving context I can imagine, has helped me to manage my own ego. It's a work in progress.

I owe a great deal to all my colleagues. We are an organization that develops the capability in individuals to influence themselves, their teams, and their results. Yet we grow through each other.

On my immediate team are the people with whom I work most closely and whose influence I can most closely measure: Barbara Gaiptman, Lisa Tomassetti, Lynne Gallacher, Suzanne Carlaw, and Sean Verhoeven. But this list should not overshadow the contribution of the other players on the HORN team. Adrienne Camilleri, for example, helped a lot with the graphics and draft reproductions of this book. Also, I caught Alan Roth stealing a glance at an early draft of this book, and upon my invitation, he was kind enough to read it and give me his considered and useful feedback. I also asked for and got great input from Lisa Young, who is in charge of the HORN Centre of Applied Measurement. But there are a whole lot of other HORN players to whom I feel grateful: account people, administrators, designers, facilitators, project coordinators. We work together in a living laboratory. We create ideas such as the ones you'll find in this book. We bounce them off each other, reflect on them, learn from each other, respond to clients who assess our creations, and respond to learners who wrestle with personal change.

I also learn about myself and the ideas in this book and feel special support from friends, both business and personal. These include people who have offered and provoked specific ideas that expanded my theoretical understanding, and my self-awareness, on the question of ego: Arnie Ein, Desmond Ryan, John Huss, Jorge Pinotti, Les Lear, and Mark Reno.

If it were not for Don Bastian, my editor, co-conspirator, and crutch — you would not be reading these words. Period.

But in truth, to really account for where these ideas have come from, I should name all the authors who have changed my world view — some of whom have been cited in this book — all my professors, my therapists, and my one-on-one coaching clients. The list is simply too long to include here.

Finally, I thank you, my reader. Your will in picking up this book, and your desire to reach even this far into its contents, is worthy of celebration. What's behind that choice of yours?

It's such humility that this book is all about.

PART I

SELF-MANAGEMENT

■

CHAPTER ONE

Ego and Self-Management

Perhaps you've seen some version of this tale:

An elder was teaching his grandchildren about life. He said to them:

"A fight is going on inside me. It is a terrible fight and it is between two wolves. One wolf represents fear, anger, envy, sorrow, regret, greed, arrogance, self-pity, guilt, resentment, inferiority, lies, false pride, and superiority.

"The other stands for empathy, truth, faith, humility, friendship, joy, kindness, compassion, hope, and love.

"This same fight is going on inside you and every other person, too."

They thought about this for a minute, and then one child asked his grandfather . . . "Which wolf will win?"

The old man simply replied, "The one you feed."

This man's wisdom rings true for leadership. Whether we run a small department or preside over a mega-corporation, we do indeed have some degree of control over which thoughts and behaviors we pursue. Developing and practicing our leadership skills precisely involves deciding which wolf to feed. That is, it involves how we manage ourselves, investing in certain ways of thinking while steering away from others.

An Hour in the Life of Ego

Is ego a big challenge in our leadership and our organizations? Consider a randomly picked hour I recently spent with several leaders.

While on my way to a meeting, I ran into a man from another company. During our minute together waiting for an elevator, he very smoothly wiggled into the conversation the fact that he ran with some people in powerful places. "You certainly know some serious movers and shakers," I said, giving him what I thought he wanted.

Walking into the meeting, I noticed one of the people present wasn't her usual sociable self. Her boss was in the room and I recalled that she seems to go quiet when he's around.

Once the meeting was under way, someone expressed worry over the status of one of the projects the group was involved in. She was promptly put in her place by a fellow who argued somewhat aggressively that there was no need for fear, because he had it all figured out.

Some tension rose later in the meeting after someone said, "I'm not blaming anybody, but if your group had managed to get the system in place, we probably wouldn't be behind today." The target of that accusation went beet-red and shot back, "Well, thank goodness you're not blaming anybody."

That garden-variety hour was revealing of how rampant ego is in the workplace. The man at the elevator was craving attention. The woman whose boss was in the room was acting submissive. One person was engaged in worry, another in dominance and pride. Another was flying in blame mode, and the last person was busy mounting her defenses.

Most people believe that leaders need some amount of ego in order to be truly effective. And most people in organizations would say, of the above behaviors, "Just another hour at the office." But this book is going to put before you the opposite point of view: that less ego means greater leadership and organizational effectiveness. That ego and its discontents do not have to typify business.

Specifically, this book will explore with you how you can get beyond ego in your leadership style. This book promises that amazing results will follow — for you, your team, and your organization.

What Is Ego?

James P. Carse of New York University offers an excellent definition of "ego" in his book *Breakfast at the Victory*. He suggests that it is the part of the individual that sees itself as above, below, or against others. This is an informal definition, yet a very useful one — one that is woven like a red thread throughout this book.

This definition requires three quick qualifications. First, this is not a book about Freudian psychology. It is not a contribution to the psychoanalytic exploration of, for example, ego's role in responding to the pressures imposed by one's appetites and conscience.

Second, we're not talking just about the person who is "full of himself," or the person who we say "has a big ego." Our position is that ego has many forms, all resulting from a deeply felt need to feel more whole or secure, and we're interested in the whole gamut of responses to personal vulnerability.

Third, getting beyond ego does not mean tamping down our creativity, emotions, principles, beliefs, and knowledge, or failing to be our real selves. All of the good aspects of our life and nature can actually enjoy greater play when our ego needs are not in the middle of everything.

The claim here is that when you feel vulnerable in some way, your ego comes out of the closet. It may manifest itself as passivity or aggression, submissiveness or dominance, preoccupation or disconnection, but it's ego all the same. Whatever its form, it makes you less effective as a leader. *This* is the sense of ego that we are considering.

For the purposes of our exploration together, think of ego as a self-centered perspective you sometimes adopt. It's the "this is about me" point of view. Ego in this sense has a primal aspect to it. It may even derive from our primal origins. Think of how wolves wrestle with the question of who's in charge. The alpha wolf, for example, sees itself as above all others. It is ready to fight or stare down in a growling contest any wolf brave or foolish enough to challenge that position. Others in the pack lower their necks to the alpha wolf as if to say, no fight here — you're in charge.

Ego occupies itself with such questions as:

- How do I get out of this terrible mess?
- Am I sufficiently in control?
- How am I doing versus others?
- Am I loved?
- Am I seen?
- Am I safe?
- Am I respected?
- Who is blocking me?
- Is this a threat to me?
- How do I get more power?
- Am I a bad person?

It's quite possible that many of your private thoughts on the job emanate from your ego. The results of these thoughts are the emotional yield of ego: sadness, fear, worry, anger, pride, hate, anxiety.

You may be surprised by how often ego reveals itself at work. Think for a moment about just one of your colleagues. Ask yourself: When does her perspective become narrow? Under what circumstances is she less creative than usual, more easily provoked, more passive or more dominant, more shameful or defensive, more aggressive, less clear in her communication?

All of these reactions are quite possibly linked to the appearance of ego.

Of course, the questions apply to you as well.

Do such ego reactions actually do you a disservice? If you are a one-person show, they may serve you favorably. There's no doubt, for example, that a certain "juice" is available to us as our ego generates its primal fight instinct.

The problem of ego in business become crystal clear when you consider how, when leaders' egos are engaged, they are much less able to:

- Hear others so they feel connected to them
- Inspire others, not by provoking fear in them, but by drawing from them their deeper motivations so they will fully engage in their roles
- Support the self-esteem of people on their team, so they see themselves, rather than the leaders, as the star of the show
- Come out of their shells in order to assert their vision and inspire their teams
- Think clearly so they can facilitate the progression of their teams toward targets

Getting Beyond Ego

Moving beyond ego doesn't mean you have to forfeit your passion. It doesn't mean you can't be a visionary. It doesn't mean dryly staying focused on the job. It simply means not seeing yourself as above, below, threatened by, or up against people or circumstances. You may actually *be* threatened, or higher up, or up against others, but getting beyond ego means you're not making it about you. And it means helping others to see it that way too.

A clear way to see the difference between ego engagement and the non-ego you is to visualize your relationship with young children. When you are relaxed and alone with a four-year-old child, you're probably not seeing the world from an egocentric vantage point. You're not trying to impress. You're not threatened. You're not trying to establish your superiority. In fact, your attention is probably on amusing or serving that youngster in some way.

In fact, we are able to observe ego in its most immature form by observing very young children. A newborn baby's orientation is that its needs are the absolute star of the show. Babies — who are totally dependent on the caregiver — are programmed to compensate for their lack of sophisticated language skills. They cry when they are hungry, they cry when they are uncomfortable. They want what they need and they know nothing else. They epitomize self-centricity.

Of course, between your birth and the present, you have matured. You are no longer all ego; you have good days and bad days, easy things to accomplish and difficult ones, all with varying degrees of ego provocation. Your self-centricity ebbs and flows.

You are not your ego. It's in there, ready to come out with the press of the right button, but it's not your identity. In Latin, "ego" means "I," but the word points more to your "self-centricity" than to your "being." You possess many characteristics that are not the total you. You possess your family orientation, your intuition, your will, your spirituality, your character, your intelligence. At any given time you manifest any one or more of these things. These are your capacities, and ego is one of them.

But when you're on the job, leading a team, frustrated that things aren't happening fast enough, or that things aren't under control, or feeling sorry for yourself, or fearful of the boss, or competing with colleagues — these are the times when your ego comes out. We're interested in getting it back in, or even getting beyond it altogether.

Getting beyond ego means managing your thoughts and personal reactions. As you'll see, it starts with knowing what triggers you. And it involves either pre-empting the ego reaction, or, if you're already engaged, redirecting your thoughts to bigger and better things.

SELF-MANAGEMENT

Are you adept at self-managing? Can you can keep away from, or disengage yourself from, the egocentric perspective?

Much evidence has accumulated over the last couple of decades that people's career success directly correlates to how well they can manage their responses. For example, research in emotional intelligence — the extent to which people are emotionally savvy, able to read others, know themselves and manage themselves — indicates that self-management skills are more important to career performance than intellectual bench strength.

You possess some skills in self-management already. When a child spills milk on a good day, you know there's frustration in the back of your mind, but you don't invest in it. You don't cry over the spill. But on a bad day, that's harder to do.

Many factors affect the extent to which you can manage your reactions. Some things are outside of your control (such as the number of milk spills before breakfast and your household milk spillage history), and some are within your control. We're particularly interested in the ones within your control. But by the end of this book, you may buy the notion that all of your reactions are manageable.

Having the ability to manage these thoughts and reactions, having the *choice* concerning them, can offer an absolutely huge benefit to a leader.

In fact, the longer I work as an educator, consultant, and

executive coach, the more I realize that self-management is a *critical task* of leaders. Your ability as a leader to align and inspire others — which is what you should be doing on the job — is either aided or obstructed by how well you manage yourself. It's as simple as that (though not so simple to do). With personal insight, frequent practice, and the advice offered in this book, you'll be able to program your own leadership style, becoming a truly influential leader.

A friend of mine is a case in point. He spends most of his social time trying to get people to hear him, like him, and respect him. It's as though he is always listening for whether he is loved, and if he doesn't pick up those cues, he busies himself generating them.

Walking with him the other day, listening to him go on and on about his current situation, I finally had to declare, "For heaven's sakes, ask me about me!" (that was my ego speaking). Loving friend that he is, the next thing out of his mouth was, "Oh, sorry. How are you anyway?" I swear that I got less than one sentence out before he jumped on part of my answer and used it to steer the attention back to him.

He's a smart, compassionate man. But he has not yet become aware of when his ego's need for attention rises to the surface.

Other manifestations of ego are similarly difficult for us to self-observe (let alone to self-manage). When we are judgmental of others, for example, we adopt a kind of "I am the judge" stance, entrenched in our belief that we are right. That too is ego. We see ourselves as at the center of the universe. From that place of pivotal wisdom, we offer our position: "This means that, and that's all there is to it!"

It is the mission of this book, then, to explain some practical ways for you to choose different, more sophisticated responses to the things that trigger you. Each part of the book moves you to greater and greater self-management and insight on your journey to egoless leadership. Part I focuses on self-management itself. Part II extends that discussion to you as an egoless leader "in the flesh" — in your interactions with employees: how you listen to them, support their self-esteem, and inspire them to greater commitment. Part III shows how it all works on a broader scale, as whole organizations are led by leaders who are constantly facilitating forward momentum, finding creative solutions to every problem and challenge that business throws their way.

Working toward this type of mastery through the insights of this book will show you how to observe and manage your own reactions, which will prompt you to choose healthy, influential responses to people and situations. This book will help you recognize how you are sometimes stuck on problems because your ego is holding you back from seeing a bigger picture; it will guide you in learning how to get beyond that stuck place and adopt an integrative, productive vantage point.

And so, to begin, let us focus on self-management. At its best, self-management is the art of moving beyond ego. It all starts with how well you know the thoughts that run through your head.

CHAPTER TWO

DETECTING YOUR SELF-TALK

It is 9 o'clock on a Wednesday morning. You have just spent an hour at your desk handling a phone call, capturing details from your voice mail, and managing e-mail messages. You're about to lead a meeting with the people who report to you.

But something is bothering you. It's Michael, one of your direct reports. The two of you were in conflict two days ago. You have not run into each other since. You suspect Michael is not over the matter. These things seem to linger for him.

As you get yourself organized for the meeting, you think about how it will go. Michael gets sarcastic when he's angry. He can be a nuisance. You shake your head as you anticipate what might go wrong.

Michael is joking with others as you enter the meeting room. It bothers you a bit. You're not sure why.

The first agenda item is the development of new productivity metrics. This is a provocative topic because compensation plans are involved.

"Shouldn't this item be put over to the next meeting?" Michael asks you, looking around the room for support. "After all, Susan is part of the task force dealing with it, and she's on vacation. It might be good if we could get her to share her insight."

There he goes; the challenge begins! you observe to yourself. You feel anger welling up inside.

Private Thoughts

What happened?

The anger rising to the surface came from your suspicion of what Michael was up to. Granted, this line of thinking may have been perfectly appropriate and rational. You may have a clear understanding of Michael and his games and your frustration may be quite understandable. But the anger you felt may also have been something you fueled, somewhat unnecessarily. You may have been reading more into the situation than was called for: your anticipation of Michael's behavior while you were still at your desk, your judgment of his joking around as you walked into the room, and your interpretation of his motives in suggesting a delay.

There's no doubt that this is how we're programmed. Our brain anticipates what may go wrong so we can protect ourselves. And it tends to evaluate how things are going in the present for the same purpose. It helps us assess things. You're probably assessing this point, or this book, right now. That's a good thing.

But the brain often errs in determining potential problems, and such errors can be costly. For example, an error can lead to needless worry. It can also lead to unnecessary tension. This happens when you become needlessly preoccupied with something. Michael, for example, may have simply been making a quite valid suggestion.

What Is Self-Talk?

There are various names for the private thoughts we have been talking about: internal monologue, chatter, inner speech. This book mostly uses the term "self-talk." Think of it as the running monologue that is accessible to our awareness.

Of course, we have many mental events that are not immediately accessible to our awareness. They happen so fast, or they are so subtle or complicated or even confused, that they don't rise clearly to the surface. Self-talk can be seen as thoughts of a higher order. Such thoughts take the form of language.

These thoughts are often a result of deeper, unconscious thinking or mental activity. It's as if they rise to the surface from the bottom of the mind. But, interestingly, we can actually impact our deeper, unconscious thinking by influencing our own self-talk. It works both ways. Our deep thoughts give rise to our self-talk and our self-talk can influence our deep thoughts. Hence the point of this book, that we can affect our thinking and, when we do this effectively, can improve, among other things, our influential leadership skills.

Self-talk can be benign, composed of daydreams, pleasant memories, and thoughts about vacations, economics, or bicycle riding. It can be right on point, sorting out plans and alternatives. It can be very productive. When your son's grade school teacher listens carefully as he recites the times tables and says to herself, "Oh, he's inverting the six and seven times-tables," that's not harmful self-talk. We're all grateful for it.

Self-talk can also be the voice of ego. It can be destructive, flowing from or reinforcing our fears and cravings and therefore blinding and deafening us to other people and what's really going on around us.

For example, at this moment, your self-talk may well be: "Is this book going to help me be a better leader? Do I buy this stuff? Does this apply to me? What's in this for me?" Since you are at the center of these queries — they are you asking on your behalf — this kind of self-talk is an expression of ego.

EXPERIENCING SELF-TALK

Indeed, self-talk is natural. It is sometimes egocentric and sometimes not. Go ahead, let yourself experience it right now. Stop reading for half a minute or so. Let the self-talk flow.

It's interesting that when you sit back and say something to yourself like, "Okay, go," there is a moment where self-talk is stalled. It's as if you're holding your breath. Your attention is on what self-talk looks or feels like, and the act of placing that attention seems to stop any self-talk. This phenomenon will arise later as we discuss the idea of managing self-talk by redirecting attention.

It's also interesting that awareness of self-talk is always retrospective. That is, when you relax and let your thoughts flow, to actually recognize this internal monologue you're having, you have to stop that flow and look back at what you were thinking a few milliseconds before. You experience the sense, "Oh, that was self-talk." We are never aware of a specific instance of self-talk at the actual moment we experience it.

This phenomenon suggests that there is an "I" who observes self-talk and a "me" — if you will — who is the self-talker being observed. And that allows for the possibility that the "I" who observes can be promoted to the role of the "I" who self-manages, who takes charge, who sets direction.

When you let your self-talk flow and your thoughts go to something more or less benign, such as, "Oh, it's time to water the plants," that's probably not ego engagement. It may be about you, if you're the one who does the watering. But the observation doesn't come from a self-centric vantage point, with you engaged in pride or fear or battle.

On the other hand, if your thoughts wander to something like, "Now I have to fight traffic. I hate traffic," then that's ego. It's not particularly germane to the typical leadership circumstance, but it is coming from what we're defining here as an ego-centric place.

Ego is the very source of defensiveness, fear, hurt, and aggression. It's the thing in other people that we have to allay. It's the thing in ourselves that we have to calm if we want to hear others clearly.

What about you? Does your own self-talk support your goals? Are you managing yourself? A good start in answering this question is to understand where your self-talk comes from and to ask whether it is serving you well.

WHY WE HAVE SELF-TALK

Psychologists have seriously pursued the topic of self-talk — intrapersonal communication — for only the last few decades. Prior to that, mental events were off limits because they couldn't be measured objectively. But the pace of research in this area is picking up steam. As evidence is gathered of the favorable impact of self-talk management on physical health, athletic performance, depression management, and self-efficacy, objectivity is entering the picture. Coupled with a better understanding of brain function through such technologies as functional magnetic resonance imaging (fMRI), this momentum has facilitated the emergence of a whole new field of endeavor: cognitive science.

One of the assumptions underlying the cognitive scientist's search to understand the physiology of thought is that many of the traits possessed by any living thing are present because they serve the being in some way. Survival is the name of the game. When a living being possesses a trait that aids its survival, then it has a better chance of living long enough to create offspring. If the offspring inherit the same life-enhancing trait, then they too strengthen their chances of survival.

Think for a moment of a bunny rabbit running through the woods. It hears a rustling in a bush nearby. The rabbit's brain has evolved to respond to this sound with a decision point: fight or flight. If it didn't have this automatic programming in its brain, the species probably wouldn't survive very long.

Other mammals have this programming, including humans. We keep an eye out for whether something is good for us (the smell of good food) or not good for us (trouble at work). And emotions like fear and anger help inform our subsequent behaviors.

Self-talk can be seen as the contribution of our language skills to this programming. The problem is that we often react with fear somewhat prematurely. The same goes for anger. In fact, the handy survival tool of keeping an eye out for what may be wrong, or what's good for us, often gets us into trouble. We reach our judgments prematurely. We emote unnecessarily.

As a species, we are learning to override this programming. A dog does not say, "I'm having a bad day and this mood is going to wreck it so I think I will choose to override the feeling. I'll start whistling; that's the ticket!" Humans can.

In a sense, the action of self-talk often also helps us save time and trouble. This is because self-talk uses previously established opinions or beliefs to interpret or judge what's going on around us. We walk around with our beliefs about the world, about what's right and wrong, and about how things ought to be. And when we see signs that our beliefs are valid, we essentially say to ourselves, "Yup, that proves it."

For example, let's say you believe that people who constantly draw attention to themselves have a big ego and should learn a little humility. You are strolling down the hallway at work and you see and hear one of the new players on your team. He's the center of attention. People are standing around him and chuckling. He raises his voice as he delivers the punch line.

You think, "Oh boy — looks like an ego problem. I can't stand that kind of behavior."

Your self-talk may have actually saved you time and trouble. After all, your experience tells you how things work, and you've seen enough. Ego problem, you can conclude. You may be right.

This piece of evidence may just do the trick when it comes to figuring out what makes the new guy tick.

You also may be wrong. For example, you may have trouble sharing the spotlight with other people because you're insecure about your position in your organization.

And the funny thing is that, at least according to this book, in the second case it's *your* ego that's engaged in this matter. He may not have an ego problem. Your own feelings have biased you.

Indeed, the beliefs that bias our interpretations are sometimes influenced by our emotions, sometimes appropriately and sometimes counterproductively. Think of worry, for example. A fellow I coach worries a lot about the financial health of his business. He's fearful that there will be a downturn in his industry just around corner. His fear practically makes him believe it's already true. When he sees headlines that even imply economic challenges in his industry, his consciousness spikes with fear. This operation of the brain assumes that it's prudent to keep an eye out in this way, but it's also overreacting and he regrets the angst he carries with him.

Of course, self-talk also addresses benign matters. It rehearses in advance of an interaction so you are less likely to blow it. It reviews what already occurred to help you process it. It recollects old memories to help you assemble new ideas. It reflects deeply on matters in order to get to the nub of a question. But underlying such meanderings is the context of self-protection.

Judgments are the focus of the next chapter, but you can see already that self-talk judges for a living, often on behalf of, or in the form of, the ego. And often it reinforces the ego. For example, some judgments that we make strengthen our sense of self. We use them to reinforce that we are right. We may say, "Things *are* the way I think they ought to be," nodding our heads as if saying we are okay. Or, "Things are *not* the way I think they ought to be," in which case the act of judging reinforces that we are okay and the thing we are judging is not. We get great payback from making our judgments.

"Yup, That Proves It"

In my work I often use what I call the Subjective Truth Syndrome (adapted from Argyris's Ladder of Inference) to help demonstrate to individuals and groups how self-talk reinforces itself and the effects this can have. The phenomenon is depicted in the diagram below.

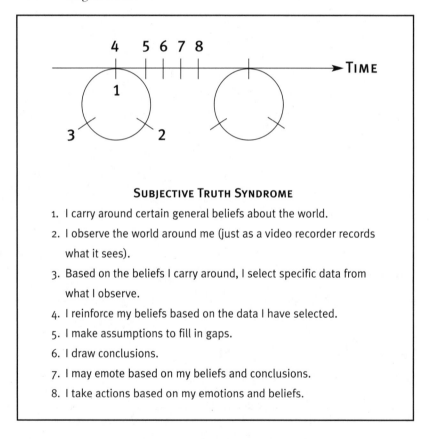

Subjective Truth Syndrome

1. I carry around certain general beliefs about the world.
2. I observe the world around me (just as a video recorder records what it sees).
3. Based on the beliefs I carry around, I select specific data from what I observe.
4. I reinforce my beliefs based on the data I have selected.
5. I make assumptions to fill in gaps.
6. I draw conclusions.
7. I may emote based on my beliefs and conclusions.
8. I take actions based on my emotions and beliefs.

Notice the diagram's horizontal line, representing the passage of time, heading to the right. The whole stretch of time shown in the diagram may take half a second to elapse. Indeed, the prejudice we're talking about here occurs very quickly. That's why it can be difficult to nip prejudice in the proverbial bud.

Each of the little circles under the time line simply represents one observation. We make an observation (items 1, 2, and 3) and as we proceed through the span of about half a second, our thoughts and bodies go into action (5, 6, 7, and 8).

The main point of the diagram is that we carry circular thoughts as we go through our lives.

What's the circularity? In order to figure things out, we refer to what we already believe. And then we say, "Yup, my beliefs were right. That proves it."

Another way of saying this is: Of all the things that could come to our attention at any given time, it's usually the things that support our belief systems that make it to the top. And then, strangely, we use these things that cross our minds to reinforce our beliefs. It's weird when you think about it. We lose interest in the truth about things in honor of our own belief system.

For example, you have certain beliefs about books like this. As you read this book, those beliefs are being reinforced. As a result, you make a judgment that happens to support your beliefs about books like this. Perhaps you believe that books on the psychology of leadership are full of psychobabble. Right now this book is talking about circular thinking, so you react with, "Yup, that proves it — psychobabble." Or perhaps you believe you have something to learn about managing your ego. This book appears to be talking about aspects of ego that you haven't confronted before, so your reaction is: "Who knows? This book may teach me something."

Step 1

The diagram starts with step 1, your beliefs. It's referring to any belief you have about any topic: beliefs about people who do certain things, beliefs that describe a certain person, beliefs about certain types of politicians, beliefs about how your friend consistently behaves under certain circumstances.

Step 2

And then there's the world in front of you. That's represented by step 2. So far, very simple. There are your beliefs. And there's the world.

Step 3

Because you've got these beliefs, they tend to bias you regarding what you observe. That's step 3 in the cycle. Your attention goes to the things about which you have some connection, some beliefs. For example, if you believe, as I was once taught to believe, that starting sentences with the word "because" is a no-no in good writing, then a sentence a couple of lines up may have caught your attention. (Sorry about that.)

Step 4

Step 4 has to do with general beliefs tending to get reinforced by specific bits of data. We're talking about the nastiness of prejudice here. The underbelly of humanity. The essence of the "yup, that proves it" syndrome. You walk around with a broad opinion on some matter, you see a little evidence that your opinion may be true, and bingo! You're more certain than ever that your opinion is true — in fact that it has been confirmed.

Maybe it's, "Great leaders have big egos. That leader over there is great and he has a big ego. Yup, that proves it. Great leaders have big egos."

Step 5

Step 5 in the Subjective Truth Syndrome is about the assumptions you make to add to the picture you're getting of a certain

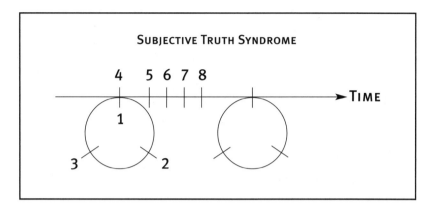

thing. You're out of the vicious circle here and back on the time line. Indeed, as time goes by, you make assumptions about the world. This too is the subject of your self-talk. In the case of the new fellow on the team, you've already concluded that he has a big ego. Then you add a new assumption: that he is going to be very interested in getting the attention of your boss.

Step 6

Step 6 pertains to the conclusions you might reach. This is also likely part of your self-talk. It could be any conclusion: I'll let the "because" thing go; that powerful, influential leader over there is too busy to speak with me; sixteen-year-old boys should not be allowed behind the wheel . . . anything.

Step 7

Of course, some of the time you become emotionally engaged by this rapid-thinking process. That's step 7. Road rage comes to mind. Or fear of being seen unfavorably. Or any one of dozens of possible emotional consequences of your natural circular thinking.

Step 8

Finally, in step 8, you may react behaviorally. Cutting the young fellow off as you shake your fist and grit your teeth. Leafing through the pages of this book to see if there's anything that looks worthwhile before slamming it shut. Walking into the new fellow's office to shake hands.

OVERRIDING SELF-TALK

It's empowering to know that we can choose to override our self-talk and our automatic reactions. The goal of *recognizing* self-talk is to then be able to *manage* it. But how? At what point in the Subjective Truth Syndrome should we step in?

The key is to know your biases and catch the temptation to reinforce them before it hooks you. Let's choose a relatively innocent topic to make the point. Let's say you are biased against stovetops because you once burned the palm of your hand to a crisp on one. You are walking around an appliance store totally resistant to leaning on all the floor models available to your tired physique. Hopefully, you catch yourself. You realize, "Oh, there goes my prejudice again. Gosh darn, is it ever unfair to label all stovetops 'dangerous.' I generalize like mad. How silly of me. These things call for heightened awareness, not disdain." Then — clear thinking self-manager that you are — you tap the top of one of the display units, verify that it's not plugged in, and start leaning. Such mastery!

Let's take some time to explore a three-step method for overriding your self-talk. This brief process would be inserted after you have observed something (step 3 of the Subjective Truth Syndrome) and before you reinforce your beliefs (step 4). A whole new world can open up to you as a result of this little process. Rather than continuing the trajectory of making new assumptions to fill gaps (step 5) and drawing conclusions (step 6), your emotions (step 7) and behaviors (step 8) may well change.

a) Stop

b) Challenge your beliefs and assumptions

c) Choose your response

Looking at the previous chart again, think about inserting these a, b, c steps between steps 3 and 4. How do you think that would help?

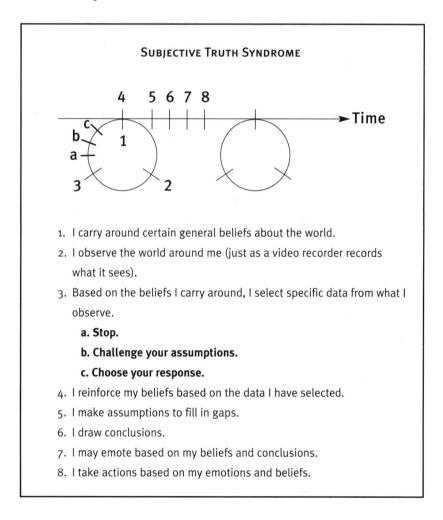

SUBJECTIVE TRUTH SYNDROME

1. I carry around certain general beliefs about the world.
2. I observe the world around me (just as a video recorder records what it sees).
3. Based on the beliefs I carry around, I select specific data from what I observe.
   a. Stop.
   b. Challenge your assumptions.
   c. Choose your response.
4. I reinforce my beliefs based on the data I have selected.
5. I make assumptions to fill in gaps.
6. I draw conclusions.
7. I may emote based on my beliefs and conclusions.
8. I take actions based on my emotions and beliefs.

For example:

You believe executives too often sweat the small stuff (step 1). Your vice president is telling you timing is critical regarding your completion of some upcoming reports (step 2).

Of all the things you could observe about this, your brain personalizes it. You perceive that she's being petty (step 3). At this point, instead of reinforcing your belief (step 4) and assuming that she is out to get you (step 5), you can:

a) **Stop** your reaction of personalizing

b) **Challenge your assumption** that she is being petty, entertaining the thought that perhaps she's got pressure above her for a better read on how the quarter is going

c) **Choose** to get the reports on her desk faster

Or consider this situation:

You have believed for some time now that your organization is cutting off its nose to spite its face, damaging quality in its rush to realize savings (step 1 in the Subjective Truth Syndrome).

At a recent day-long meeting of sales directors (step 2), the vice president has announced (step 3) that he wants you and your peers to take at least part of a sales territory yourselves, "to keep your hand in what this company's all about." Stop yourself from moving to step 4 by:

a) **Stopping** the urge to get annoyed and resent them for expecting you to manage the team and work like a team member at the same time

b) **Challenge your assumption** that head office is just trying to squeeze more sales out of the sales department

c) Choosing to look at getting back in the field as an opportunity to identify more closely with the reps under you

It can take a lot of practice, but it is possible to raise your awareness of when your automatic responses are taking over. The solution is to engage the following template in order to redirect yourself.

An event takes place that could trigger an automatic reaction.

a) Stop

Resist the temptation to react without thinking. Consider the facts of the incident, event, or change, not your self-talk about it

b) Challenge your beliefs and assumptions

After removing yourself from an emotional response, ask yourself, "What opportunities does this event, change, or incident present me with?" Be as objective as you can. Challenge yourself to see the situation from all possible perspectives

c) Choose your response

Once you've considered your options, choose your response. You may still respond the way you normally would have, and that's okay. By pausing and considering before acting, however, you consciously choose your response, rather than allowing your "hardwiring" to choose it for you

As you practice thinking this way, you'll remember situations in which your self-talk created an automatic response in you. Gradually, you'll be able to recognize counterproductive self-talk and pretty much change it on the spot.

But here's what we're most interested in at this point: how overriding our automatic responses helps us to be influential leaders. The idea is that our automatic responses often represent the voice of our ego. These responses are busy defending us. They dictate our judgments of others. They make us combatants when we need harmony. However, when we can sidestep the robotic, we open ourselves to the possibility of being more genuine.

Let's get a little deeper into this topic by looking at the types of judgments we make when our ego gets engaged. This will elevate our ability to self-correct.

CHAPTER THREE

Managing Your Judgments

"Results," Karen said during her first coaching session with me, "are *everything.*"

A senior leader at a large food-distribution company, Karen was frustrated. She thought several members of her team were not taking the organization's near-term sales targets seriously enough. She was quite worried about her numbers for the quarter.

"How do you know these employees aren't taking things seriously?" I asked her.

"Well, they just don't look stressed enough," she said. "I mean, we're just about in crisis mode. They are always joking around at meetings. They waste time doing administrative things when they know they should be shaking the trees. I have spoken to them about it, but they just don't get it."

Karen said that this sort of attitude seemed to be spreading throughout her department. She admitted that the pressure was beginning to manifest itself in her health. She'd had a headache for five days running. Her sleep was disturbed. She was a wreck.

"Is there a different approach you could take?" I asked. "Is it possible that you need to be less judgmental of these employees?"

THE PARADOX OF JUDGMENT

Paradoxically, one of the chief tasks of leaders is to judge — without being judgmental.

My comment to Karen lit a fuse, and she nearly exploded. "But I'm a leader — it's my *job* to judge!" she said. "I care deeply about hitting our numbers. Not only does it affect my compensation, but it also reflects on my career. And my pride. I'm in this to win! It's my job to drive these guys. I have to watch every nuance of their attitude and behavior. Our success depends on the quality of my judgments."

Obviously she was right: judging *is* one of the most important tasks of any manager or leader. No company can survive if management loses its focus on results. Failing to assess employee behaviors and making sure they fit the organization's larger plans would be suicidal.

But as we will see in this chapter, there's judging and then there's judging. Understanding *how* we judge will help us make sound judgments that bring real results. As in the case of self-talk in the previous chapter, it's a matter of sound self-management. We will focus here on a dangerous kind of self-talk: making judgments of other people.

JUDGMENTS ARE NOT ALL CREATED EQUAL

We make judgments all the time, and that's okay. The problem crops up when our factual judgments become generalizations and personal attacks. It's the difference between finishing the first apple of your life and declaring, "I didn't like that apple" and moving on to saying, "I don't like any apples" and moving even further to "I don't like your apples."

Generalizations and personal attacks are often, but not always, the result of egos becoming engaged. Ego is the part of the individual that sees itself as above, below, or against others. When you are in this mode, you are more likely to generalize and personalize your observations. Doing so helps you to protect yourself in some way. If you feel like you're up against another department, for example, you'll likely be tempted to take a fact or two and generalize. "See," you declare, "these guys are all like that."

In the example above, Karen observed, "Some of my key people were joking at the last update meeting." That's one kind of judgment. It is factual. But Karen couldn't resist the temptation to run with that fact and add:

- "These guys are goofs"
- "They're not taking our numbers seriously"
- "Things are falling apart"

In these examples, Karen's brain is taking something factual and extending it.

We do this all the time (or perhaps I should say, many people do this often). We see a couple of things go wrong and we assume that everything is falling apart. Somebody in my office walks by wearing flip flops. Somebody else passes my door wearing a tie-dyed t-shirt. I care a reasonable amount about professionalism, so my head twitches as I think, things are out getting of hand around here; I definitely have to address this. I speak to our office manager about it and she says: "No, it's not a problem. They're going on a team-building adventure today."

Oops.

Why do we do this?

The Subjective Truth Syndrome explored in the last chapter partly explains the mechanics of it. Things come to our attention because they are important to us. We quickly assess whether they are the way we think they ought to be. We reach our conclusions and judgments accordingly.

We suggested in the last chapter that we would be smart to challenge our beliefs and assumptions. We also suggested there that this method of operating on the world saves time. Rather than running around verifying all of our assumptions and conclusions, we extrapolate. We don't have the time to be thorough. We use a small amount of data to reach sweeping conclusions. It serves us very favorably. The problem we are exploring is how that judgmental momentum can trigger the leader's ego, leading to employee disengagement.

We have to reconcile the paradox of needing to judge while not being judgmental. We can do this by learning to focus on an individual's behavior and not the individual herself. This is sometimes difficult to do.

There is a whole community of psychologists who argue that the extent to which a person moves from a specific observation to a general one correlates with degrees of pessimism or optimism. According to this theory, pessimistic people are more likely to interpret one bad thing as a sign of other bad things. For example, when a pessimistic sales leader hears about a sales opportunity being lost to the competition, he is more inclined to catastrophize. "We're doomed!" he might declare. An optimistic leader, on the other hand, might be more likely to see the misfortune as localized.

The point, for our purposes, is that regardless of why you may be tempted to reach negative judgments, it is prudent to ensure that you keep your ego out of it. Recognizing distinctions in the different kinds of judgments you make may help you do so.

TYPES OF JUDGMENT

Let's distinguish between three types of judgment: factual, extended, and personal.

- A *factual* judgment is a statement of what we know to be true. "You have been late three mornings in the last two weeks." This kind of judgment is usually safe to make

- An *extended* judgment is a generalization we make from some specific examples we have seen. For example, somebody walks in late a few times and you say, "You tend to be late." Or you try to create a spreadsheet and find it difficult. You have found it difficult before. So you declare, "Spreadsheets are always so complicated!"

In these two examples, you can see that there may be a grain of truth to the claim. On the other hand, such claims are not necessarily true. Therein lies the risk. This kind of judgment should be made cautiously. When they are offered carelessly, they can lead to irrational conclusions or even prejudice. When you catch yourself making extended judgments, or when you hear them from others, try asking whether the sentence is actually true. For example, "Do two occasions of lateness really constitute a tendency?" Or, "Are *all* spreadsheets complicated?"

- A *personal* judgment is a label or generalization about a person. Examples include:
    - "You're late for everything"
    - "You are basically intellectually lazy"
    - "He's a very loud person"
    - "He's never accurate"
    - "You're just not very good at that kind of thing"

Personal judgments can be invalidating, hurtful, and dangerous. They should therefore be avoided.

Leaders are susceptible to slipping into personal judgments — that is, to judging their employees rather than their behaviors. Spoken aloud or acted on, this kind of thinking de-motivates employees, shrinking their self-esteem. When they detect that you are thinking this way (after all, they judge too), they can generalize about you in a way that can permanently damage trust.

A judgment is "personal" if:

- It uses a generalization such as "always," "never," or "only" in reference to a person ("You only stay late when I do")
- It assigns personal ownership to some disliked thing ("Your argument is flawed")
- You would be hurt by it ("You are not committed to this project")
- It labels the person ("You are a cold person")

WHAT'S SO BAD ABOUT PERSONAL JUDGMENTS?

It's undesirable to utter sentences that are received as personal judgments. They may be extended judgments but be interpreted as personal, such as when you say, "You tend to be late." The consequence of personal judgments is that they often make people feel "smaller." Their self-esteem may drop for a while. Until it rises again, you're going to get lower productivity. You may also face other problems, such as people adopting a contagious negative attitude.

So we're saying you have to watch what comes out of your mouth.

Of course, it's not so easy to always control what you say. Lots of times, you are emotionally engaged by your judgmental self-talk — your ego is engaged — and getting a grip on how you're acting is difficult.

Recall the Subjective Truth Syndrome in the previous chapter. After our self-talk goes through its little circle of reinforcing its belief, we move into behavior mode. That is, we start making new assumptions in order to fill in the picture we've painted; we make some new conclusions; we emote; and we go into action.

For example, let's say you believe that the senior leadership of your organization has no viable strategy. It's like there's nobody up there driving the bus. You get a communication announcing an upcoming change in policy. You perceive change as a perfect example of what you've believed all along: there is no strategy. "After all," you think, "this change in policy is going to take us backward, not forward. It will undo exactly what we've made great progress on through very hard work."

Okay. That's the cyclical part. You interpreted in your head that the change supports your hypothesis. "Yup, that proves it. There ain't nobody driving the bus."

From this stance on things, you add a new assumption: "I bet they didn't talk to anybody before they made this call." And you move to a conclusion: "My boss is not respected enough for them to want to ask." Time for some emotion. You shake your head. Your jaw closes tightly. The phone rings. You pick it up. You say nothing except a loud, cold, "What?" It's not like you. But that's what happened.

Let's talk about this.

First of all, that's not you getting beyond ego. That's you with ego fully engaged. Your self-talk took you to this place and it left you with relatively strong feelings. Those feelings are about to bleed into your next conversation.

Bingo. This is the point.

Your ego is the part of you that sees itself as above, below, or up against others. In this case you see yourself as below (or above!) others. Perhaps as a victim of others. Your attention is not on implementing the policy change, preserving the progress you made on things so far, or on who is on the other end of the phone. It is on you.

For simplicity's sake, let's recognize that there are basically three components to this situation: the facts, your opinions of the facts (generated by your self-talk, of course), and your emotions (an outcome of your self-talk). I like to separate out the emotions from the opinions because it allows us to further distinguish what's okay and what's not okay in the quest for allowable judgments.

So far we have said that factual judgments are fine to make. We said that extended judgments can be risky. Personal judgments, of course, are not okay. And now for the point: Judgments that produce negative emotionality are poisonous. We're talking about blame.

BLAME

Most people I know think two things about blame: that a "blame culture" is undesirable, and that sorting out where things went wrong, even to the point of who did what, can't be so bad.

Similarly, as I see it, blame has two components: the claim that points to the cause of something that went wrong, and the emotion that is embedded in the claim. If Karen blames her team members for being late, her judgment goes well beyond the facts that they were late and that being late is not okay. She adds the emotional component. This is precisely how factual judgments morph into personal ones laden with emotionality. Let's look at this more closely.

In our coaching session, Karen defended her blaming behavior by saying, "But they were goofing off; and goofing off during periods like this is *not* okay."

"The fact of goofing off is true — on this occasion," I responded. "And goofing off is not okay during times like these — as a rule. But why all the intensity?"

As we explored this question, we discovered that the emotion she was feeling about the department's numbers was making her see behavioral patterns and attitudes that weren't necessarily there. It was a short step for Karen to move from seeing the facts to blaming her employees for them. She was insecure about how she would be perceived if she missed her numbers. Her ego was totally engaged and it negatively influenced her ability to lead her people. Her judgments did her a disservice.

Indeed, as we continued our sessions, Karen saw that she was actually putting herself and her goals in danger. We explored how easily this kind of emotion, when it comes from a leader, can create a blame culture. Sometimes just one spark of blame can set a whole department or organization ablaze.

"No way," you may argue. "Emotions are good. I'm a passionate person. I believe in what I do. I *love* what I do."

That's fine. Emotions are not ego. They may be a result of ego. When you're responding to a threat and you get angry, that emotion of anger is coming from your ego. But when you're looking at a sunset so beautiful that it brings tears of joy, it's not about you, it's about the sunset. It all depends on who is the star of the show; if it's you, it's ego.

I'm not suggesting that we should try to eliminate all emotion. I love emotion. Our emotions bring us our deepest wisdom and joy. Strangely enough, they even guide our rational thought. After all, emotions inform our values and our values inform our goals. And the efficient route to a goal participates in the definition of what is rational. Emotion is good.

But when as a leader you take your emotions out on someone, those negative feelings are going to hurt the person. You're not going to inspire the person with this behavior; you're going to make them fearful. Blaming is counter-productive.

There are some proponents of systems theory who argue that there's no such thing as blame; there are only communication problems. This rings true for me. Think of someone you have blamed for something that went wrong in your life. Now ask yourself whether improved communication between you and that person could have prevented the problem. In this sense the blame is as much yours as that other person's.

For example, a former colleague and I parted on bad terms. I'm tempted to blame him for leaving me high and dry. But I know in my gut that if we had been communicating, we would have worked things out and he would have left gracefully. He blames me for being a meanie. If we had been communicating openly, he wouldn't have to do that.

In any case there's never really one single cause of things. When you start tracing things back, you usually find a whole array of causal factors.

When you're trying to improve a system, sorting out causal factors can be beneficial. When what you're really trying to do is find someone or something to blame, this quest is damaging. In the latter case, the intensity you feel is your ego getting involved.

DETECTING AND ADJUSTING YOUR OWN JUDGMENTS

Let's say you are a service manager. One of your employees enters the room complaining that the salespeople have been making promises that can't be kept.

You shake your head and say to the employee: "Those people in sales just don't get it, do they? They make messes and we have to clean them up. We have a reputation to protect and they are blabbermouths. You can't run a business on lies. They're always overselling. I can't stand it."

Then you pick up the phone and call the guilty party and make it crystal clear that you don't respect their attitude toward the truth and the health of the organization.

Of course, as service manager, your mission is to please customers as much as possible. The sales force, in contrast, has the job of painting the best picture possible in order to get as many sales as possible. You don't want people lining up with complaints about a product because it doesn't do what the salespeople said it would do. They don't want to feel that you aren't going to back up the product that they're selling. This is a classic tension built right into many organizations' systems. Senior people often just say, "Let them battle it out." They believe that if both sides do their jobs, things will work out.

The problem is that in the scenario described, you are actually hurting yourself and others. By being so aggressive with your counterparts in sales, you are alienating them. And alienated salespeople are less successful in making sales.

So what would be smart to do next time?

1. Remember that when you are deeply immersed in your emotional response, you're not even aware of what you're doing until some time passes. When you can catch an objective wave, ask yourself, *"Is this going to help me get what I want in the long run?"* If it will, then go for it. If you conclude that it won't, then it's time to manage your self-talk.

2. Either during the conversation with the "guilty" department or in advance of the subsequent conversation, ask yourself, *"What is my self-talk here? What am I saying to myself?"* Here's a clue: When there is anger, the word "should" is embedded in the self-talk. Perhaps you find running through your head the words: "Somebody should harness these salespeople." Recognize that the self-talk is fueling your anger. Say to yourself, "I am not this anger." Repeat that a few times until the meaning of the words sinks in. At this point you will probably notice some dwindling of your intensity.

3. After detecting the connection between your intensity and your self-talk, you can rephrase things for yourself: "Salespeople need to know what can and can't be done so they can effectively manage customer expectations." With the revised self-talk engaged, you are liberated to effectively communicate that service parameters can be established and agreed on. A lot more effective than declaring war.

To summarize, certain judgments get you into trouble because they hurt your relationships with others and are counterproductive. These are the kinds of judgments that you can feel yourself making. They come from an engaged ego. They are accompanied by the emotional aspect of blame. You can get beyond this engagement by overruling your self-talk. You can literally reprogram your brain, on the spot, in order to manage your affairs.

This is pretty amazing. It separates humans from other animals. We can actually manage our reactions. Dogs and cats and rats and cows can't do it. But we can.

STICKING WITH THE FACTS

The field of cognitive science has much to offer to this approach. In fact, cognitive therapy is based on the notion that by looking closely at our beliefs, we can affect things like our mood and perspective.

Here's how it works. Let's say you are feeling sad or depressed. You try to figure out what belief seems to accompany or underlie that feeling. By assessing whether you actually stand behind that belief, you manage to break yourself free of the feelings it caused. Or by reframing that belief, you actually change the feelings that connect with it.

So you're not just catching yourself being judgmental and amending your self-talk on the fly in order to avoid muddying your relationships with employees. You're becoming your own therapist.

Let me tell you about my wife, Joan, to whom, by the way, I have dedicated this book.

Joan's stance on these matters, at least when they apply to her, is, *Hogwash!* She is a passionate woman, an artist, as a matter of fact. And a loving wife, tremendous mother, and a giver of affection all around.

Joan's view is that when she's upset, she's upset. She's not interested in anyone suggesting that she could modify her upset mood. Doing so is absolutely counterintuitive to her. It's *her* mood, for heaven's sake! When she blames me for once again not emptying the dishwasher, she's very aware that she's angry. She wants me to know she's angry. And she's being perfectly clear and overt in her judgment.

She's not interested in optimizing my morale in honor of the team's productivity. She's not interested in the possibility that I didn't empty the dishwasher because I was attending to other matters. She's not interested in the irrationality of her claim that I *never* empty the dishwasher. As a matter of fact, when I don't empty the dishwasher, I *am* a lazy, inconsiderate slug.

The upshot of all this?

Who am I to say that she ought to manage her ego? That would be judging her. That would be my belief system referring to itself to prove her wrong. That would be my ego defending itself.

If I were beyond ego, I would not judge her. I would empty the dishwasher.

This book, in other words, is about you. It's not about what others should do differently; it's about how you can do things differently. Its claim is that it is highly advantageous, in a goal-oriented environment, for you to get beyond ego. Stick with the facts. Be informed by your feelings, but don't be blinded by them.

You may be curious about how someone with my view of the damaging effects of unharnessed negative emotionality in the workplace could survive with someone as passionate in her expression as my wife. Just know that after she expresses herself, hears me apologize, and gets just a little coaxing, she resumes her loving ways with ease. It would not be unusual for us to be engaged in the dishwasher dispute one minute and be dancing across the kitchen floor the next.

THE PARADOX OF INFLUENCE

In concluding this chapter, let's return to Karen's point — that judging is job number one for leaders. We discussed how her point raises the paradox that as leaders, we must judge constantly, yet to be good leaders, we must be rigorously non-judgmental. A related paradox is the Paradox of Influence: The more we want something as leaders, the less influential we are in getting others to give us those things.

The psychologist Carl Rogers writes that "the major barrier to mutual interpersonal communication is our very natural tendency to judge, to evaluate, to approve (or disapprove) of the statement of the other person or group." Indeed, our tendency to judge and evaluate hinders our ability to communicate *and* our ability to influence.

This is an ever-so-subtle tension for each of us. As leaders we want something from our employees, yet if we are too assertive or aggressive in trying to get it, we throw off the balance — and we don't get it. We may even come across as being arrogant or self-centered. We're trying to influence the employee in order to get our own way — but the only way to get our own way is to set aside our thinking about what we want.

When, for whatever reason, managerial insecurity sets in, ego kicks into high gear. We scramble to make judgments about the source of the problem, and we try to force a solution. Our tendency to be self-oriented has a negative effect on our ability to influence.

It's easy to see how our judgments block us from being influential:

- When we make personal judgments — or, speaking more broadly, value judgments — we strengthen our sense of self. We bolster our ego by telling ourselves either "Things are the way I think they ought to be" or "Things are *not* the way I think they ought to be, but I'm okay and the thing being judged is not"
- This energized sense of "self" makes it difficult to empathize
- When we don't empathize, people don't listen because they don't

feel heard

- When people don't listen to us, we are not as likely to influence them.

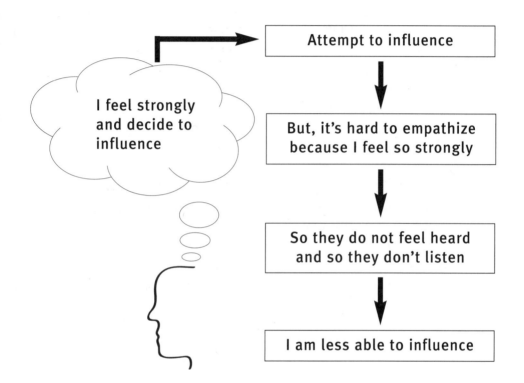

Does that mean as a leader you should throw out your objectives and spend your days patting people on the back and making them feel loved? Not at all. Rather, you can integrate into your goal-oriented style the insight that comes only from paying genuine attention to the other person. And that depends on your self-management: your ability to detect your self-talk and judgments.

The key for Karen proved to be realizing that her judgments about her employees' attitudes were preventing her from being an effective leader. When she confronted them with the opinion that they were "late all the time and didn't take things seriously," they were understandably hurt and angered. Her approach served only to increase the distance between her and her team. It became very difficult to talk productively about business outcomes.

Once she began to understand her own insecurity about her ability to drive the department's success, she was able to:

- Keep her ego out of the picture
- Think factually about her team's situation
- Listen to her staff

And what did she find out when she talked to them about this again? That her three team members had made a pact to quit smoking and to go to the gym on their break. This explained their slight lateness and their high energy. Pushing her ego and personal judgments aside, she congratulated them on their initiative. Then, with a feeling of lightness that surprised her, she got back to the task at hand: getting the organization's numbers up.

CHAPTER FOUR

BEING REAL

My goodness. What would an egoless you look like? Is it really possible? Are you really being real when you reach this state?

In chapters two and three of this book we looked at two key ways to manage yourself on the way to becoming a highly influential leader:

- Recognizing and learning to manage your self-talk
- Detecting and getting control of your judgments

When you do these things, you do end up being more effective as a leader. You listen better, because you've managed self-talk's intrusion on your listening. People feel more connected to you and thereby readier to follow you. You are better able to motivate them because you are in touch with their needs and you are less likely to make them feel "small" through your judgments. Managing troublesome self-talk and its judgments — managing your ego — makes for better leadership.

When you are less encumbered by the effects of your ego, you are better able to see the world for what it is.

For example, Billy was late for the weekly meeting two times. It is what it is. It's not a sin; it doesn't foreshadow doom. It may not mean he was a bad hire. And you may be wasting a lot of your energy entertaining that as an issue. The question is what, if anything, you're going to do about it.

When you're listening to Billy explain his reasons for being late, are you pre-judging? Is your self-talk intruding, keeping you from focusing on what the man is actually saying? Are your judgments invading your connection with him?

Again, there are the facts about Billy, and there are your opinions about the facts.

THE FACTS OF THE MATTER

It's important to distinguish between facts and opinions as clearly as possible. They are very different animals, though we often confuse them. For example, when you have a strong opinion about something or someone, doesn't it feel like a fact? When someone is prejudiced, don't they behave as though their beliefs are not up for debate? When someone has offended you, don't you feel absolutely certain that you've been wronged?

Our opinions often dress up like facts. But they are not. As we saw previously, they are self-generated things. They don't hail from the outside world. We manufacture them.

Most of us would agree that operating in the world in a way that is easy, effective, and satisfying is the way to go. In this chapter we'll look at a variety of different ideas that support or articulate this point. We will:

- Differentiate facts from opinions in a slightly technical, philosophical way — one that points to the difference between objectivity and subjectivity
- Look at one man's view of where real human happiness comes from and see how it involves letting go of self-talk altogether
- See how one tennis pro suggests we can best approach tasks: by finding the zone where there is no chatter in our heads
- Consider briefly how driving a car while chattering away to yourself

highlights two different levels of mental activity: the real you is the one doing the driving, while the one who's doing all the thinking is somewhat of an intruder

- Discuss a kind of mental posture you can adopt as you approach the world: looking forward and making your visions come alive rather than dwelling on the past and self-talking your way out of your future
- See how when you let go of your ego's need to self protect, you can afford to fully disclose, communicating things that your ego previously held back

A LITTLE PHILOSOPHY

Most of us see philosophy as something that's easy to drown in if you get in too deep. So let's just dip our toes in the water.

In this book I refer to the real world, the facts of the world, as though they are all objects. For example, Billy is an object. After all, you can physically touch him. But I also refer to other facts as objects — for example, the fact that Billy was late two times. It's not something you can touch, but it's "objective" just the same. For our purposes, it's an object.

I refer to all the thoughts and opinions of the objects in the world as the "meta level." The term "meta" is a perfect fit here. It refers to "one level higher." What's one level higher than the objects of the world? Our opinions about the objects.

So we have two different realms: a realm made up of the objects of the world, and a realm one whole step removed from those objects and made up of our opinions.

Here's a helpful way to understand the difference between facts and opinions. Let's hearken back to our high-school grammar lessons. (Am I dating myself here? Do they still teach grammar?) Take the sentence "I like apples." Recall that "I" is the *subject* of the sentence, the entity that does the liking. "Apples" is the *object* of the sentence: the things being liked. Similarly, or accordingly, the apples are in the object world while the "I" that's doing the liking is on the meta level, the subjective world.

So Billy's lateness, assuming it's true, is in the object world. Your opinions about and judgments of his lateness are on the meta level.

Ego operates on the meta level. It pretty much spends its time asking the basic question, "Are things the way I think they ought to be?" Your ego generates its opinions as provocative moments pass. If you're at a meeting and someone from another area makes a remark about your team that you find offensive, the remark itself is in the object level. Your reaction to it is on the meta level. (The discussion of the Subjective Truth Syndrome in chapter two describes all of the meta-level activities, ranging from which words you select from the words the person utters about your team, to whatever emotion the matter evokes.)

There are two ways in which this book is helping you get closer to managing your meta-level chatter:

- First, by helping you understand more about the workings of your consciousness. This will increase your ability to self-correct. Self-correction, or self-management, through higher self-awareness is a key to being a better leader

- Second, by helping you interact with people in ways that get you into a non-ego momentum, making you less likely to evoke ego in others

We won't likely ever be masters

Keep in mind that we can't shut the meta level down permanently. At least I certainly don't know of anybody who has accomplished this. There are probably lots of people, you included, who regularly find themselves, for hours at a time, immersed in their work, even with other people, without any ego involvement of any kind. But as for living in the world without any ego, I doubt it. My dog can do it. (Yours can too.) But not any people I've met.

There are millions (and millions) of people who learn meditative techniques in order to quiet their self-talk — and, thereby, their ego. For many of them, it's a lifetime mission. There are lots of movements that promise to be the best or only way to such a nirvana, but I've never seen any evidence that one particular road actually works best in terms of mastery over self-talk.

Psychotherapy can help people process the unresolved matters that excite their egos. In this way they increase the length of time that they can remain ego-free while, let's say, on the job. But psychotherapy could go on forever. There's always another layer of the onion of angst to peel off. You can get closer to perfect mental harmony, but never quite make it in a sustained fashion.

People mature with time, and many of us, often with the help of others and even books like this, end up becoming more passionate yet less likely to be provoked by others or turns of events. We end up learning some of the grace or interpersonal finesse to minimize how often our buttons are pushed. We are never perfect, but we do get better.

So let's look at how you might think and behave in an egoless state. A state in which you:

- Become less and less encumbered by feelings of insecurity, pride, and self-defense
- Are more and more likely to experience the joys of being "lost" in the real world, the way we say we are sometimes "lost in wonder" or "lost in joy"

Flow

You may have heard of the concept of "optimal experience," or "flow," laid out by the psychologist Mihaly Csikszentmihalyi in his book *Flow*. Here is a man who is writing about true human happiness. He says you are optimally happy when you're in a state of flow or in the zone. There is no ego when you are in this state. In fact it involves a loss of the feeling of self-consciousness. You're just immersed in activity, as though the current is just carrying you along.

You've probably had this experience. Perhaps you have fallen into flow when you played a sport. Actors find flow. Doing house renovations can yield the experience. Ironically, you can transcend normal existence by getting down to earth.

What about the application of this type of flow to our jobs? Here are the main conditions required for flow to be experienced. We must:

- Have a goal regarding the matter in which we are engaged
- Be challenged by that matter
- Be concentrating on what we're doing
- Have a good measure of the skills called for in order to achieve the goal

You're not likely to be in a state of flow when you're doing something too far above your skills. And you're more likely to exit such a state out of boredom if what you're doing is too easy for you. Your mind will wander from your task because you will stop concentrating on it.

The effect of being in flow is profound. Chatter stops. That voice in your head that's forever thinking, judging — it's not there. Ego, with its fears and desires, its worries and preoccupations — it's not there.

What *is* there, then? Only the thing being attended to. The stuff of the object world. It is an experience of total immersion. An experience in which action and awareness are one. When it's over, we wonder where the time went. We may not remember every detail of the experience, but we know very well that it was pleasurable.

It's funny how when we are experiencing flow and we ask ourselves whether we are in flow, *poof!* it's gone. It's as if we're chasing our tails. We experience enjoyment and when we reflect on it, the enjoyment disappears and we have to chase it again. Around and around we go until we're dizzy.

The Paradox of Flow

We've all experienced the Paradox of Flow: that the state of flow disappears when we consciously try to get into it. Everything is going along fine, and then self intrudes looking for some happiness. As it does so, it is cut off from it. There is no room for ego in happiness. There is only room for being.

I hope I haven't made it sound hard to have this experience. It's not. It's easy. As I said, undoubtedly you have already experienced it in your life. Most people I speak to about it have it much more in their private life than at work. Some examples:

- Some of us are hard-bitten gardeners. We grub around in dirt for hours on end. Like kids reluctant to leave their neighborhood games, we have to be coaxed in for dinner. "I *am* hungry," we remark as we're cleaning up for our meal. "I think I must have skipped lunch"
- Others of us see a golf course when we close our eyes. And when we're actually playing golf, the golf course is all we see. Eighteen holes of forgetfulness. Eighteen holes free of worry
- A really weird example is what a friend told me once. He said that he attains this frame of mind when he works to clean his apartment more quickly than he did the time before

The moral of the story is that this experience of flow is what you're headed for as you label your problematic patterns of self-talk and judging; increase your management of these meta-level thoughts; and understand more accurately what triggers you so you can pre-empt your robotic reactions.

You can experience life with far less intrusive self-talk. You can find joy. There is joy in doing. It is not in achieving. It is not in results. It is in execution. It is in doing what any living creature does: living.

Fear of flowing

You may, like many people, find the idea of a "flow state" or an "egoless you" a little strange or even scary, especially in a work situation. You may wonder, "How do I create flow if I'm not in the picture? Without my ego taking care of things, won't I get myself into trouble? Without ego, where is my will? Don't I have to be really disciplined and careful in order to get things done and avoid making mistakes? Won't I be too easy-going and unfocused to be effective?"

When we're in flow, are we capable of goal orientation and compassion? The answer is yes. We are hard-wired for both. Our ego interferes with, rather than helps, our ability to focus and to empathize.

The rollout of flow on the job starts with your management of your self-talk. Redirect it to what others are saying when they are speaking, rather than letting it wander. Redirect it away from sweeping judgments and to the facts. Move conversations toward goals that stretch you. The experience of flow, and your heightened performance as a leader, will unfold quite naturally.

A GAME OF DOUBLES

On this topic of redirecting conversations toward goals that stretch you, keep in mind that we're programmed for goal achievement. This is how the brain's left hemisphere operates. The brain is like a heat-seeking missile. Just as such a weapon reads the temperature ahead of it and self-corrects its trajectory in order to get closer to the hotspot, so your brain detects and moves toward its goals. When you know your goal well, have it clearly visualized, and keep out of your brain's way, achieving the goal will strangely take care of itself.

It's as if the goal gets transmitted to some underground operations center in your mind. The prime activity of that place is to constantly monitor what your senses are picking up and, based on the primary mission, send signals to your conscious mind regarding how to behave.

This is exactly aligned with the thesis of Timothy Gallwey, expressed decades ago in his great book *The Inner Game of Tennis*.

Gallwey proposes that we have two selves, Self 1 and Self 2. He shows how Self 1 gets in the way of a good game of tennis. Self 1 is the equivalent of what we have termed ego. It is very busy judging your last move and trying to control your next move. After a shot, it might yell, "That was dumb — you can't win like that!" In response to a serve — as the ball is coming at you — it yells, "Nice and easy now!" (as if that admonition is going to do the trick for you).

Self 2, on the other hand, is what Gallwey proposes we allow to take control. Self 2 is you without self-talk. It's that operations center, handling things to the best of its ability.

Let's weave these ideas together a bit. Gallwey's Self 1 is what we want to disengage from. It's a bunch of meta-level activity that presents the image of being grounded in the real world but that is, in fact, one whole step removed. It judges. It criticizes others and itself.

Gallwey's Self 2 is you in the flow state. It's you dealing purely at the object level. The facts of the world are at your disposal, and you are trusting that your body and unconscious mind are handling them to the best of your ability. Self 2 knows the goal and it deals with the facts in a way that gets you to the goal.

Indeed, Self 2 will do your job to the best of your ability. It can't do magic, so getting your ego out of the picture doesn't guarantee you career success. As Gallwey argues, you still have to practice your serves. But without the encumbrance of ego, you can at least do the best you can.

DEFENSIVE DRIVING

Visualize what it would look like to function in your role in a way that's consistent with operating from Gallwey's Self 2 or in Csikszentmihalyi's state of flow. Is it possible to operate without ego, without a judge in your head trying to get out from underneath, or keep its place on top, or win the battle?

Picture yourself driving across town to see a friend. You're driving along, making all the correct turns, letting other drivers in, slowing down, speeding up, responding to traffic lights and road signs.

If you're like me, while these things are happening, you're busy having other thoughts. Oodles of them. They are not likely about driving. They are about anything and everything. They may or may not be egocentric thoughts. But there are a lot of them.

Now do the math. Subtract all the thoughts running through your mind as you were driving, all that self-talk, and what do you have left? You have what life would be like without a sense of self. Just observing the objects of the world and responding to them. Self, it could be said, is an add-on.

In a sense we have just described the experience of mindfulness. Driving along and keeping your mind on the driving. Such a state does not mean you are free of thoughts or observations or intuition. It means you are directing your attention to what you are doing. There is no ego present. No sidebar, no unrelated and intrusive self-talk. No private personal judgments. Busy? Yes. Productive? Yes.

Of course, driving is conducive to self-talk because, once we're experienced at it, we pretty much can do it on automatic pilot. Our consciousness has leftover bandwidth for other things. So we fill it. Indeed, the flow experience, as we said, requires some degree of personal stretch or challenge. Hopefully, in your leadership role, with challenging goals, you don't have this problem.

IMPROVING YOUR MENTAL POSTURE

It can be hard to imagine being an influential leader without bringing a great deal of ego into the job. Mobilizing a department to meet a project deadline, for example, takes an awful lot of pushing. Most people believe it takes a big ego to wield all that power.

And yet we've all spent time in the offices and cafeterias of companies where something quite different is said about ego in leadership. Perhaps you've said or thought some of these things yourself:

- "James is a smart guy and works hard. He's very determined. But the organization has ground to a halt since he was hired. He has a big ego, all right: he's a micro-manager with a finger in every pie. Everyone who works for him is frustrated, humiliated, and paralyzed. They all know that it doesn't matter how smart he is or how high his standards are: he's so afraid of making mistakes that nothing can ever get done under his watch. He's insecure and trying too hard to be perfect, and his ego is blocking the company's progress"
- People are starting to treat Abbie as irrelevant because of her ego problems. Abbie has risen to the top of her company's human resources department over a period of ten years. She likes to think of herself as a mother figure at her office. She is very proud of this role. She's very friendly and calls everyone by name. She gets pleasure from projecting this image. As a result, she has lost credibility in the eyes of senior management. They see her as someone who represents the front-line employees as opposed to someone who facilitates smooth relations between those employees and senior leader-

ship. Her desire to make friends and be seen as central to loving
relationships on the job — her ego — has intruded

How many times have you heard it said that someone is talented and could really go places except he lets his ego get in the way? It's true. The real secret to reaching our goals is to set ego aside and focus on the task at hand.

You may further counter, however, that there are a lot of very big egos who have made it to very big places in the corporate world. Indeed, sometimes the power of their personalities, their ability to inspire fear in others, their strong belief that their way is the right way, their tendency to control in order to make their way *the* way, their willingness to work like mad in order to achieve their goals, all conspire to create one mighty strong leader. Wouldn't removing the ego of such leaders do them and their organizations a great disservice?

This has not been my experience. It's true that most of the folks who fit this description don't actually *seek* the help of a coach. In their opinion, they're already fine the way they are. But I and other coaches have coached plenty of such people who have been *sent* for help. The desired result in these cases is consistently achieved as they reduce their arrogance and lighten up on their temper and the desire to control — tempering their egos. People around them become less fearful — and more respectful of their vision as leaders.

Optimal leadership is about placing one's attention on making things work. It is not about temper tantrums, angst over things appearing out of control, fearing what might go wrong, stressing over looming, unreachable targets, attributing blame, getting engaged in turf wars. These things come from leaders who are busy interpreting, looking at what just happened, or what happened some time ago, and getting engaged in it.

Looking back, looking forward

Ego keeps us tied to the battles of the past and prevents us from dedicating our energy to keeping the peace today and tomorrow. Have a look at the following diagram.

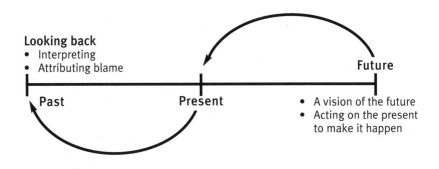

Looking back
- Interpreting
- Attributing blame

Past   **Present**   **Future**

- A vision of the future
- Acting on the present to make it happen

My belief is that most people tend to operate on the left-hand side of the diagram. They are in the present, of course. And they are frequently glancing to the past — either the immediate past or the mid- and long-term past — and evaluating what they have just experienced. This is where they get engaged.

For example, somebody who has just heard of a new policy change may angrily exclaim, "I'll tell you why they made this new policy; it's because they . . ." It can also lead to a quest for blame, as in the case of someone chatting with a buddy about some catastrophe that just happened: "Do you want to know who's responsible for this? I'll tell you who's responsible for this. It's . . . !"

Of course, some of this retrospection is necessary. Historians would roll in their graves if we concluded that we shouldn't learn from the past. The question is how long we spend there. I know some folks who define mental health by that duration. The healthier we are, the faster we move on. Some believe that glancing back, and resting in that backward glance, leads to physical health problems.

A smaller percentage of the population tends to operate on the right-hand side of the diagram. They have a vision of the future and they are acting in the present to fulfill it. They declare what they are going to do. They are asking others for help. They *act*. These are people who get things done. For them, the future is coming at them. They are like a winning tennis player, for whom only the current point matters — this shot and the next one and the next one.

THE JOY OF FULL DISCLOSURE

As you operate in the world with the future coming at you, making things happen, your style of communication will change. You will become a great listener. You will be less inclined to blame. You will be more likely to address the needs of the people around you. You will also have a greater willingness to put your cards on the table, because you will be less weighed down by the meta-level demands of egocentric interpersonal relationships.

If, on the other hand, you see your boss as somewhat unpredictable, then you may fear saying what's on your mind. If your colleague is likely to be hurt or angry, you may be very reluctant to say that it bugs you when she speaks too loudly. If your employee is somewhat volatile when being criticized and you happen to strongly dislike confrontation, you may fear a showdown.

These are all examples of your self-talk doing you a disservice. This is how ego shows up on the job. What would it look like to be free of this mental activity? It would look like self acceptance (without the arrogance that can sometimes go along with that). It would be Self 2 communicating about matters relevant to productivity in a non-judgmental, non-provocative way. It would be you with nothing to hide.

Let's say I want to suggest to you that you read this book as thoughtfully as you can. Let's assume I have some data indicating that you are not doing this right now. My stance, of course, is that there is a lot of meat here that you're skipping over on a hunt for something a bit more appetizing. Let's see what I might offer.

The point of this exercise is for you to see that when you have nothing to hide, you can afford to say things that you have been too frightened to communicate. There are three components to this method of communication:

1. The point you want to make to the other person
2. The genuine reasons why you are reluctant to make the point
3. The reasons why they may not like the point

All three of these things call for bravery. But it's bravery that is easily accessed when you are not ego-ridden. After all, when you know the goal, it's a shared goal. The point you want to make to a person helps to get to that goal, and you're not overly focused on all the softer issues surrounding that point. So you really have nothing to hide. You can get it all out there. In honor of the shared goal, you can get someone to embrace the point.

Furthermore, and beautifully, you are much more influential when the other person realizes that you're coming from a place of achieving shared goals, rather than from a place of politics or fear or anger. In fact, you are respected for your authenticity and your objectivity.

It's time for me to make my point about how you're reading this book. Hmmm. How shall I say it?

Well, first of all, I don't want to offend you, in case you decide to permanently set the book aside.

But, hey. I have nothing to hide. I'll just put it all out there. I won't just say what I want you to do. I'll put it *all* out there. I will give you my best impression of what may be on your mind.

Together we'll get all the issues out. Believing that I am coming from a sound position, but humbly being willing to be wrong, I will lay it out for us.

Regarding how you're reading this book, I get that life is busy for you. That the times you skip over stuff may be a result of your mood or other matters preoccupying you. Perhaps you're feeling lazy. Perhaps you don't really embrace or accept what you are reading. Maybe the writing is not clear enough. It's also possible that it is just not interesting to you. Or maybe you've never been a good reader and I should feel thankful that you've made it this far. Any of these may be true. And they are all okay with me. I get it. Who am I to judge you? I glide through some books too.

I also feel funny saying these things to you. I get that it's a little forward of an author to suggest that readers modify their approach. It's a little presumptuous of me to assume that you're okay with what I'm attempting here.

I also feel pretty sure that that, with this book, if you go too quickly, you'll miss some key stuff. Others who have learned about these ideas have reported a slight but tangible elevation of awareness that ultimately led to a markedly improved leadership style. I know from experience that slowing down and digesting one section at a time — perhaps with a highlighter — can help you to get the most out of this material.

But . . . you decide. I only want you to hear my plea. Obviously the choice is yours. I must earn your respect, your trust.

That's it. How did I do?

If I had been feeling insecure at the time of writing these things (insecurity: ego engagement, rampant self-talk, Self 1 chattering away, non-flow state, meta level gone wild), then each sentence would have felt risky.

But you know something? I really do have nothing to hide. I took a full-disclosure approach to this communication. I accept myself enough to know that I'm okay with whatever decision you make. I don't feel arrogant about it. I accept you regardless of your stance on the matter. You're okay in my book.

The point? When you get into a zone of egolessness, it's all okay. You accept your honest opinions for what they are. And you can use a full-disclosure style of communication as a vehicle to keep clear of your own fears. It actually helps the person you are speaking with to stay out of their own ego place when they hear your non-judgmental approach.

"Yes," you may say, "but you have no skin in the game in the case of my slamming this book shut. You have no one person in particular in mind when you say these things. It's low risk."

"My vision is to get leaders to be more influential by exposing them to these ideas," I would reply. "I'm on my way to doing that. I am okay. I don't need skin in the game to pursue this vision. And even if we were face to face, I would still not judge you for however you are making your way through this book. But I would still advise you to slow down, use a highlighter, make notes. I would still take a full-disclosure approach with you."

So how then do you argue with your boss using this full-disclosure approach? You preface your point with an honest statement about your reluctance to counter argue.

How do you tell your colleague you wish she would lower her voice? You mention your reluctance to tell her and you point out that you get that it might be an intrusion to raise the topic. You're raising it because you want to sort things out.

How do you criticize your volatile employee without getting into a battle? You disclose your reluctance to come on too strong and you explain how, that being said, your eye is on making things run smoothly.

These approaches have a few things in common. One is that in each case you are exposing your own vulnerability. You are indicating that you understand how the other person may judge you unfavorably. And how you don't want that to happen. This minimizes the ego response of the other party. Most importantly, each approach creates a context for your own brain: there is nothing to hide. When the whole truth gets out there, it will be clear to everyone that your focus is neither on your self-talk nor theirs. Your focus is on the facts against the backdrop of the mission.

EGOLESS LEADERSHIP

What does all this have to do with you and your leadership responsibilities on the job? A lot. When you learn to manage your chatter and judgments, when you are therefore focused on the real world, dealing with the facts that are coming at you, you are able to see your task and those around you so much more clearly. You save so much time and energy because you're not trying to do two things at once: your job and the job of doing what your ego is delegating to you. You can go about your business accompanied by a sense of joy.

Imagine yourself living this willful, compassionate, and authentic life: making peace with your fears, relaxing your judgments, staying focused on the facts. Visualize the possibility of the true you, insecurities transcended, facing the future with presence of mind. Isn't it obvious, and exciting, how this is going to make you a more influential leader? Isn't this going to help transform your workplace into a place where people are working together with commitment, ego-free communication, and compassion, with joy infused in task orientation as they reach synergies peacefully together?

PART II

SELFLESS MANAGEMENT

CHAPTER FIVE

DEMONSTRATING EMPATHY

We're switching gears in this part of this book. In the previous four chapters we considered you and your self-talk without getting too much into the dynamics of your relationships. Now, we're looking at those dynamics. Indeed, self-management skills are most called for as we interact with others. In this and the following three chapters, therefore, we will focus on your activities as an egoless leader: how an egoless leader actually works with employees. We will focus on how egoless leaders demonstrate empathy, draw on the wholeness of others as they discuss goals, draw on the source of engagement in employees by supporting their self-esteem, and inspire commitment.

As we start down this path, ask yourself this major question: "Do the people on my team feel that I know them?"

This is not as simple as asking whether you do in fact know them. That's a skill in itself. But we're going further than that. Ask yourself whether they *feel* that you know them.

Getting your people to feel connected in this way is one of the keys to effective leadership. When people feel heard, understood, known, they feel connected.

I am a great believer in the idea that built right into human life is a feeling of aloneness. It was in Erich Fromm's book *The Art of Loving* that I first heard of this notion. The day before we are born, we are about as connected or whole as we can get: we are inside our mother's womb, basically experiencing unity. Then we are born. Things change in a very big way. We are separated from that experience of wholeness. Disconnected. We spend the rest of our lives seeking that reconnection.

There is reason to believe that the role of ego in the personality is to find some version of that reconnection. In this context, not having that wholeness makes us insecure and the job of ego is to compensate in some way. Ego is a regulator, responding to threats and trying to retain and get more of what it already has. Finally, when it's satiated or just feeling safe, ego recedes.

Thus your role as leader is to compensate to some extent for the ego needs of others — their need to be heard, to be supported, to be protected.

You must be genuine about it. If you fake it, the truth will out. It must be regular, pretty much in the fabric of your relationship with each of your team members. With this bond set in place, coupled with your vision of the future, you will exceed your highest expectations of leadership effectiveness.

One thing for sure: Your employees will benefit from the sense of connection. Feeling wholly understood by you will not only grant them partial relief from their existential aloneness, it will also elevate their self-esteem. You will empower them to greater heights of personal success.

The person being touched is not the only winner. You will benefit too, because the toucher also feels the connection. Aside from that, when you know where your employee is coming from, you will undoubtedly learn new things. Discussion will ensue. Progress will be made.

Oh yes, and productivity will be elevated.

The extreme opposite of this philosophy of leadership is the fear-driven relationship. That's when you don't give a hoot. You just expect or demand what you want. This approach is dehumanizing and, over time, either a real productivity killer or a cause for plummeting morale or even mass exodus. Our goal here is just the opposite: to help you develop the skill to touch people with your clear understanding of their perspective.

It's not that you have to yield to their perspective. One of the things we'll explore is how to stand your ground while still taking them somewhere they may not initially want to go. For example, you may want to redirect their efforts and they may object. You need to skillfully show that you very clearly understand their objections and that you still plan, perhaps after further explanation or even collaboration, to implement the desired change.

Causing your team members to see that signal of "I can completely identify with where you are coming from" involves self-management on your part. It involves the skill of making them the star of the conversational show, not you or your ego. You have to be able to manage your self-talk and the judgments hidden inside it in order to make this work.

Of course, you do that to some extent already or you wouldn't be where you are today. On a bad day you don't do it as well as on a good day. And you don't do it as well with obstinate team members as with people you are closely aligned with. In this chapter we simply want to raise the bar.

THE PARADOX OF SELF-MANAGEMENT

It's a little strange, don't you think, that the key to managing others is to manage yourself? We are bumping up against the Paradox of Self-Management. The facilitators from my own team and I see this paradox come to life each time we help groups develop their leadership and coaching skills. Folks walk into these learning sessions basically thinking that they're going to learn how to get other people to follow their lead, to get them to do things differently, to get them to do what they want them to do. But they leave the session owning the dictum, "For change to occur, I must change."

The good news for them is that what they seek is all within their control. Things are simpler. Whereas there were once multiple people over whom to gain compliance, now there is only one.

The bad news is that you have decades of previous programming to manage. Your self-talk, your ego needs, your habits regarding judgments all come from decades of practice, role models, and conditioning. Thank goodness experience shows that great headway can be made.

You may be beginning to see that at the heart of this book is a philosophy of total personal accountability. We've already suggested that your reactions to people are driven not by them but by your own beliefs. We've also said that, though we may be tempted to blame others for our misfortune, our own inability to communicate ought to be seen as the primary culprit. We're about to suggest that your ability to connect with people is a function of how able you are to shut off your self-talk and listen. Later, among other examples, we'll look at something interesting: how, in the same way that we empower employees to make choices by elevating their self-esteem, we ourselves become agents of change in the world rather than victims of limitations when *our* self-esteem is heightened. All of these claims link to the Paradox of Self-Management: we own the changes we want to cause.

"That's all very fine," you may say, "but *how* do I motivate and inspire my employees?" It starts with demonstrating empathy to them, which is the topic of this chapter. It then flows on to aligning their goals and your goals, which is the subject of the following chapter.

Demonstrating empathy is the art of making people feel fully heard.

THE LISTENING GAME

The psychologist Carl Rogers came up with a wonderful tool, a listening game, which trainers sometimes play with their participants to give them first-hand experience of empathy. It's a somewhat scary or threatening game, but it can be very instructive. Consider trying it with someone you know well, maybe even an employee. I play it with my wife.

Let me explain the game by describing a recent professional application. A little later I'll propose that you try the exercise on your own.

I was asked to help a senior leader resolve a problem between two employees. One of the troubled people was a manager; let's call her Brenda. The other person was Brenda's subordinate, Christine. Brenda and Christine hated each other, not to put too fine a point on it. In fact, their animosity was so profound that the senior leader said that if we couldn't fix this problem, Christine would be fired. (He believes in protecting his managers.)

So Brenda, Christine, and I went into a room alone and played the listening game.

My role was that of facilitator. The rules are simple. One person says something to the other person, something honest about the relationship, and lasting no more than thirty seconds. Then the other person paraphrases what was said, starting with the words, "I hear you saying . . . ," until the first person is satisfied that what she said was wholly heard. When that's done, the roles are switched, so both parties get to communicate what's on their minds.

I invited Brenda to go first. Here's how the conversation went.

"Christine," Brenda said, "when you come to work in the morning you've got a scowl on your face and you don't say hello to people. It's unfriendly and it wrecks the morale on my team. And I don't like it."

"Brenda," Christine responded, "I hear you saying that you don't like me and you never did. You think people don't like me, and I think it's you they don't like."

I asked Brenda, "Is that a one-hundred percent accurate depiction of what you tried to say — yes or no?"

No surprise here. Brenda said, "No."

"Okay, Christine, try again."

Interestingly, Christine couldn't do it. So we got Brenda to repeat her statement. After a few tries, Christine finally satisfied Brenda that what she had said was wholly heard.

Then it was Christine's turn. Despite the fact that she was speaking to her manager, she was to say exactly what she felt.

"Brenda," she said, "I hate how you talk to my colleagues about me behind my back. I don't trust you and nobody else does either. I just don't like you."

Poor communication skills are not reserved for employees. Brenda also had to have the statement repeated. But ultimately, Christine got heard too.

The game went on like this for a few more rounds. Initially, it was a perfect example of how we don't listen. Brenda and Christine couldn't seem to hear each other at all. Our empathy skills, particularly when we are on the defensive, are not so hot. Rogers was right when he wrote that our judgments interfere with our ability to listen. Imagine what an on-the-job conversation between these two co-workers must have been like!

And yet as the game continued, Brenda and Christine were beginning to "wholly hear" the other. And while each of them had many months' worth of accumulated fear, hostility, and suspicion to contend with, their communication styles were beginning to soften. They were starting to feel more comfortable in each other's presence.

Sympathy vs. Empathy

We've been talking about empathy. What is it and why is it so important?

The best definition I've seen for the word "empathy" involves the notion of identifying with someone. "I empathize with you" means "I can identify with you." It means to see things from the other person's point of view.

When you empathize with someone it doesn't mean you agree with them. It only means that you can see where they are coming from. You can take on their perspective for a moment.

Empathy also does not necessarily mean that you take on the person's feelings. Adopting someone's feelings may result from empathizing with them, but not necessarily. For example, suppose you told me that you are having trouble concentrating while you read this book because you are preoccupied with stress from your job. I, for one, could empathize with you in terms of having had the same circumstances interfere with my own concentration. If you tell my wife the same thing, she might actually feel some of your angst. She probably wouldn't "run with it" or exaggerate it, or let it knock her down, but she would let some of the feelings in. Both of us would be empathizing.

This actually points to the difference between empathy and sympathy. They are not the same. If someone is grieving the loss of a loved one, and you express your condolences but you're not in any way doing any grieving over this loss yourself, you are *sympathizing* with them. You are removed, standing on the sidelines. You care, perhaps, but you're not experiencing their feelings. You are not identifying with their feelings. Sympathizing with them is a fine thing to do, but it's not empathizing.

But there is another version of sympathy. It's when you let in so much of the feelings that you end up making the other person's issue more about you than about them. This too is not empathy.

Empathy is somewhere between being emotionally disengaged on the one hand and overly emotionally engaged on the other. Empathy is the skill of allowing yourself to have feelings but not so much that you become egocentric.

Effective communication with employees calls for more than sympathy. Empathy is a necessity.

The diagram below illustrates the distinction between sympathy and empathy. Let's say someone tells you about the loss of a family pet. This news evokes a level of emotional response in you registering at some point on a horizontal line representing degrees of feelings.

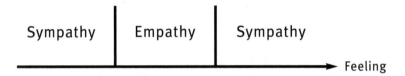

At the far left of the line are the minimal feelings you might have in response to this, perhaps motivating you to simply acknowledge the bad news. ("I'm sorry about Spot.")

On the far right of this line are the extreme feelings you may have in response to the news. Perhaps you end up on the floor, hopelessly banging your fists, weeping over the loss. In this case, you're more emotional about the matter than Spot's previous owner. You've got some stuff of your own going on.

Both the far left and far right reactions represent sympathetic feelings. On the left is simple sympathy, as in what we express by sending a "sympathy card" in the mail. On the right is sympathy exhibited by, for example, war sympathizers — taking up the cause. We're interested in the middle. It's a skill to stay there.

As we said, your goal as a leader is in the middle of the two extremes: the delicate balance between allowing yourself to feel someone else's feelings and totally holding onto your own outlook. In other words, empathy means you neither patronize someone over what you have heard nor become so affected by it that you lose sight of your own goals or even the other person.

DEMONSTRATING EMPATHY

Now that you have this clearer understanding of empathy, put your ability to "hear" to the test. This may be harder than it sounds.

Find someone now with whom you can play a version of the listening game that Brenda and Christine played.

The topic can be just about anything, so long as there are strong feelings involved: local traffic woes, an argument that they are in the middle of, what they don't like about you, or life. They need to speak for about half a minute. What they say has to be honest.

When they have said their message, start your response with "I hear you saying." Notice the present tense of that phrase. It's not "I heard you say"; the idea is to establish a sense of sharing in the present.

According to the home rules for this game, they need to assess whether they are wholly heard on a feeling level as well as a logical level. For example, if you get all the facts right but do not make them feel that you are connecting with their emotions, then you are not making them feel wholly heard.

Also, you don't need to get all of their details back to them. You only need to give them the details that matter to them.

It may seem unfair to have a rule that requires you to get the right details without being able to ask about them. But that's a key point! If you are an effective empathizer, you will sense at some level what's important and what's not. (Remember Self 2?)

You have to pick up both verbal and non-verbal cues, listening for words as well as thoughts and feelings not expressed in words. You have to shut down your own self-talk by managing your thoughts and focusing attention on listening to the employee and making them feel heard.

The key is to listen for the speaker's feeling, above all else. Concentrate on:

- Detecting and identifying with whatever feelings may underlie what they are saying
- Not judging the person
- Seeing the world from that person's point of view
- Actively listening
- Stopping your own self-talk and attending to the person
- Showing genuine interest in them
- Creating a safe environment for them

What this game tests is your ability to manage your self-talk. This means you must not let yourself be too self-oriented — too focused on your own thinking, your own goals, your own ego. When these things happen you tend to connect with others a little less effectively. The question, and the challenge, is whether you have the *habit* of stopping what you're doing and investing yourself in the person communicating with you. Doing so is important — it will help you understand what the person is saying. More than that, you will cause the person to feel heard. And the person who feels heard is much more likely to listen to you when it's your turn to speak.

We said earlier that empathizing does not necessarily imply that you pick up on someone's emotions. Yet we have also said that when you are listening, you are best to listen for feelings. Both of these things are true. Sometimes a speaker is not expressing feelings; they are giving you their perspective on a matter and your job is to see it their way. But if feelings are involved, then optimal empathy means you're capturing — feeling — those feelings as well. After all, feelings are part of their point of view, and it's that point of view that you need to capture.

But, as indicated by the feelings line in the diagram above, the extent of your emotional engagement will come in degrees. Some people seem to have more ability to connect with feelings than others.

My experience is that men are most challenged by the skill of the first vertical line in the diagram, the line that depicts the ability to let some feelings into awareness. I have trained hundreds of groups of people in empathy skills, and from that experience I can say with confidence that males are generally less inclined to let feelings into their consciousness during a dialogue than women are. The females of most species are hardwired for emotional connection. If they can maintain a connection with their young offspring, they are better able to help them survive.

Women are more likely to have the opposite challenge. Indeed, it can be very challenging for them, when they're on a connection roll, to shut off their feelings and stay in that middle space.

As you would guess, I have seen oodles of exceptions to these sex-based distinctions, so don't take anything on this matter too personally, please. My desire is simply to help you have a broader context from which to see what is going on when you confront challenges.

But sex is not the only factor. Culture, familiarity with the person you are connecting with, your attitude toward the person, your commonality with the person, your current emotional state, the extent to which you are in touch with your feelings, your mood that day, brain chemistry, habits — all of these are factors too.

Indeed, one's empathy skills come in degrees. Some leaders are better at it than others.

The key is to try. My own experience is that when you actually take on the attitude or true point of view of the other person, you can open doorways to emotional connection. It starts with identifying with their point of view.

MANAGING WITH EMPATHY

Okay, now that you're mastering the game of making others feel wholly heard, let's turn up the volume a bit. Let's consider you as leader.

My prediction is that empathizing is tougher for you than it looks. Why? Because:

- It means that you have to focus more on the employee
- It requires you to set self-talk and ego involvement aside
- It seems unnatural — like most people, you want what you want
- It involves thinking about the employee and your own goals at the same time

Are you in touch with your people? Can you feel the mood of a roomful of employees and capture that mood in your remarks? Equally important, can you be face to face with any one of your employees and feel what they are feeling? Can you do it when you're disappointed with the person? When the person disagrees with you? Empathy is much tougher when you're not in agreement. Are you effective in dealing with individuals when their opinions differ from your own?

Empathizing, particularly when you are being challenged, requires that your ego be held in abeyance. When you see yourself as above, below, or up against others, the notion of letting their perspective into your consciousness is counterintuitive.

Let's look at how to respond to employees when there's tension between you. There is a two-step dance for handling those awkward moments. The first step involves empathy: causing the person to feel heard. The second step involves offering your response: helping the person to see your point of view.

The challenging part is step one. When someone is pushing your buttons, it is difficult for you to put that aside and listen. As we said, it's counterintuitive. But it's rational. It helps fulfill our goals. Let's take a moment to look at these two steps.

Step 1

As a leader you find yourself in this situation frequently:

- Assigning a task that you know the person won't like
- Offering criticism to someone who you predict will get defensive
- Dealing with someone you don't get along with
- Dealing with employee disputes
- Giving bad news, such as telling someone that they didn't get a promotion or that they've been laid off

It is when the other person is confrontational that management is more difficult — basically when their opinion conflicts with yours and they're stubborn about their opinion.

Of course an employee's tendency to stand up for their rights, to speak their mind, to disagree is not a bad thing. Indeed, whole political systems are based on two parties being in opposition. We'll talk much more about this in the last part of this book. It's healthy because two heads are better than one. Somebody has an opinion. It leads to someone else taking the opposite side. They work things out, thereby reaching a position that integrates both points of view. The use of empathy makes resolving tension easier, come faster, and feel better.

So, step 1 involves you empathizing with the person. This means that you actually try their perspective on for size. You identify with their point of view. Let in their feelings. Paraphrase what you heard them say and get them to verify that they feel understood. Now it's time for step 2.

Step 2

This is when you integrate into your empathetic view the focus you have as a leader on your goals.

Although there are as many possible situations out there as there are leaders, let's consider just one.

Marilyn, a branch manager for an insurance company, wants an employee, Jim, to finish up some critical record keeping for a senior-management meeting the next morning, in advance of next week's audit of their office.

Marilyn knows that Jim isn't going to want to do it — he had been grumpy about staying late one evening the previous week to finish up details pertaining to a new office initiative. Marilyn could ask Nancy, but she's been spending evenings for the past week at the hospital tending to an ailing parent. Jim is sorry, more or less, for Nancy, but he doesn't think it's fair how he keeps getting saddled with extra hours.

Marilyn approaches Jim and says, "Jim, I'd like you to work late again tonight."

Visibly upset, Jim says, "I can't tonight. I've made other plans. Sorry, boss."

Marilyn says, "Well, there's nobody else. Nancy's tied up taking care of her father, and we've got to be ready first thing tomorrow to prepare for the audit. I've got an advance meeting early tomorrow with the auditors. So I'm sorry, but I need you to do it."

Jim's voice gets a bit louder: "Come on, Marilyn, this isn't fair. I've had to do a whole lot of extra stuff lately and I don't think I should have to do this. Last time I did this you forgot to leave me the security code for locking up and I didn't get out of here until midnight. Give me a break!"

Marilyn has shown a tiny amount of empathy when she said she was sorry, and she appealed to Jim's nice-guy side when she said she needed him to do it. If she gets her ego engaged, however, she may say, "Tough. An audit can be a career maker or breaker, my friend. Welcome to the real world. You'll get your share of exceptions. But tonight, you're working late. Okay?"

In this case, Marilyn has been firm. Her self-talk probably is,

"Don't talk back to me, buddy. I'm in charge here." Jim's confrontational response has caused his manager to get defensive. She really does see herself as up against the enemy. This is ego in its growling form.

What's so wrong with Marilyn's approach? you may ask. Life is like this, right? Sometimes managers have to be firm.

Maybe. However, even if Jim does stay late tonight, he's going to resent it. Tomorrow will probably see extra tension in the bank. Perhaps the tension will go away. But if Marilyn's style doesn't change, she may ultimately deplete the energy level of her employees. They may feel less empowered, and their self-esteem could slowly decline. The office's sales and customer service levels could be affected, as a result. If headquarters ever decides to lop off some local offices from the organization, theirs could be one of the first.

Let's look at a slightly more balanced, more empathetic approach that Marilyn could take.

"Jim, I know you feel there's an imbalance here, and you're right. You've been doing more than your share of last-minute preparations for meetings. And staying late last week was a favor. And having to stay extra late because of the problem locking up was a real drag. So my asking you to stay late all over again has to feel like you're being taken advantage of. Right? But we're in a jam here. If you were in the same situation as Nancy, you'd expect me not to interfere with your hospital visits, I'm sure. And I do have to make it to the meeting with the auditor. I can't think of another way to handle this situation. Yes, it's a real drag. And it's got to be done. Okay?"

In this case, Marilyn has tried to capture the essence of Jim's feelings. The more accurate her depiction of Jim's perspective, the more powerful the empathy gesture will be. She's taken essentially the same stubborn position, but probably will have fewer negative consequences. Jim will feel heard. The empathy has an ameliorating effect. Reality is still the same — Jim has to work late — but steps have been taken to reduce the resentment.

Of course, if Marilyn really wanted to reduce the resentment, she would work out a deal. Maybe Jim could take off for a few hours now in exchange for having to work tonight. Maybe Marilyn could explain to Nancy the way Jim feels and will agree to do something extra for him. There are many possibilities. The point is that Marilyn's low-empathy response had the effect of shutting things down. She got what he wanted in the short term, perhaps, but she still shut things down. The high-empathy, more other-oriented response would lead to a better resolution.

Did Marilyn's empathy gesture looks artificial to you? Was it a con job? My opinion is that it's only slippery if it's done with slippery intentions: that is, if Marilyn's self-talk, is "I can schmooze this guy and get what I want, then this will be done." On the other hand, if Marilyn is truly listening to Jim, honestly getting in touch with how her employee feels, then she is being straight.

First we empathize. Then we lead. That's a handy tool. Empathize, then lead.

The worst-case scenario is that you'll have to rethink your position. That can't be so bad — after all, it is your position and you're doing the rethinking. The best-case scenario, the one that surprisingly is most likely to occur, is that the other person will feel touched by you. They will feel heard and understood. Then they will relax, and be open to your input.

MORE ON FULL DISCLOSURE

Here's a good way for you to infuse empathy into the culture of your team. When you're not sure of what someone has just said to you, don't ask them to repeat it. Instead, ask something like, "Can I tell you what I heard you say and you tell me if I'm getting it right?" And then try your best to say what you got.

What does this do?

When you consistently show this gesture, people appreciate it. They pick it up for themselves. It sends a signal to your team that everyone — you included — is responsible for listening. It puts some skin in the game for listeners because rather than asking people to repeat themselves, they are risking revealing that they have not listened. Finally, and perhaps obviously, it facilitates better mutual understanding, because it implements a listening protocol.

I have seen this one new habit transform the culture of teams.

Telling someone what you heard them say doesn't mean that you forfeit your position. On the contrary, it means they'll relax as you proceed to explain your position. You'll be heard as you tell others your way of seeing the world.

CHAPTER SIX

Drawing on
the Source of Goals

By now you may be visualizing incorporating more empathy into your leadership communication style. Sometimes this will mean that you simply have to redirect your digressing self-talk back to what someone is saying to you. Sometimes it will mean making the more challenging effort of overcoming your egocentric stance concerning the person or their message.

Either way, the good news is that empathy certainly doesn't mean forfeiting your goals. That, of course, would be a problem. After all, the ideas of leadership and goals seem to go hand in hand. Smart leaders know where they are heading.

However, goals, by definition, have not been reached yet, so they give rise to a natural tension. As we saw in the last chapter, when this tension is rich, ego comes to the surface and makes listening difficult. It makes you see yourself as up against something or someone. But when you see this tension as a river of opportunity flowing toward you, things go much better.

Regarding this tension, I remember saying to a very wise man that I felt conflicted over goals. On the one hand, I told him, I was trying to live in the present, without ego, enjoying the moment. On the other hand, I was working in a very goal-oriented environment where achieving more was the name of the game. The two goals conflicted.

This man snapped me out of it. He described an enlightened gardener, kneeling in his garden, carefully pulling weeds and patiently pruning his plants. This gardener, he said, lives very much in the present, mindfully working away. But he also has a vision for how he wants his garden to appear. He is operating in the present to fulfill his vision.

Frankly, I felt pretty stupid after hearing this simple explanation. Though the conversation took place about fifteen years ago, it is quite possibly the main inspiration for this book. We can operate in the present, beyond ego, and still be heading somewhere.

WHAT ABOUT ME?

But who is driving the bus? If we're this egoless leader, where is the hunger to achieve? Where is the teeth gritting, eye squinting, growling, snorting beast that wants what it wants? What happens to *me* when I forfeit my ego?

Good news! It depends. If your goal is well visualized and embedded in your unconscious mind, you're in good shape. Don't forget, we're assuming in this book that you have two parts. The first part is the one you may be most familiar with. It's at the level of your self-talk. It's your ego, seeing itself, for example, as up against challenges, as above others, or below others. In Gallwey's terms, it's Self 1. It's your wandering mind while you're driving along. It's the part of you that judges for a living, assessing whether it likes what it sees.

The second part of you is what's underneath the surface.

Research shows that the conscious mind operates at the speed of about 40 bits of data per second. That's about all the bandwidth you can handle. It's not much. For example, if you put your attention right now on your right foot big toe you will notice sensation there (I hope). But with everything else going on, your conscious mind doesn't have room to keep those sensations present in your attention. It keeps that stuff underneath.

Also underneath are your skills, attributes, knowledge, habits, intuition. And that's just the soft stuff. There's also the programming for all of the millions of activities taking place in your body at this very moment. For example, your brain, as you read this material, is probably processing its attack on various viral, fungal, and bacterial infections going on inside you. Your conscious mind just doesn't have the space to think about these things. I've heard it estimated that the stuff of which you are totally unaware is clicking along at the rate of fifteen million bits of data per second (yes, that's a ratio of 40 to 15,000,000).

For me, the really funny thing is that we have the illusion that our conscious mind is in charge of things. But there is all sorts of evidence that this is not the case. Initial research was done in this area by Benjamin Libet. He showed that there is actually a half-second delay between the unconscious mind and the conscious mind. In other words, each time you think you've decided to do something, it was actually decided by your unconscious mind about a half second before that point.

If you think about it, this line of thinking causes all sorts of philosophical problems. Free will, for example, comes into question. If your conscious mind slams this book shut but it was actually your unconscious mind that made the decision, then doesn't that put the conscious experience of choosing into question?

However, it's not our mission here to wrestle with the philosophical implications of these ideas. What's important is for you to understand that your conscious mind doesn't have the bandwidth to accommodate all the machinations going on in your head and that it's your unconscious mind that plays a huge role in how you handle yourself. Self 1, the judge in your head, is an intruder on the tennis court. Self 2 — that's who we want playing the game.

You are at your leadership best when you can get your ego, your judge, to relax. Let the bigger, practiced, skilled, able-to-handle-what's-coming-at-it you do the job. This is the part of you with the insight. Malcolm Gladwell's recent book *Blink* speaks to this. He points out that, in the blink of an eye, we can "thin slice": we can make rapid assessments of people and situations. First impressions work this way. From some processor deep in the unconscious, we quickly size things up.

That's the place we have to get your goals embedded. When your goals are clearly visualized and embraced in your unconscious mind, you can actually afford to operate in the present with confidence that your empathy skills, for example, won't throw you off track.

How do we get our goals nicely tucked in down there?

EMBEDDING YOUR GOALS

Defining your goals helps. Writing them helps. Publishing them for all to see certainly puts some skin in the game. Making sure they inspire you must make a difference. Having multiple goals for different parts of your life — financial goals, career goals, family goals, physical goals, humanistic goals, personal-interest goals — ensures that you are treating the matter of being goal-oriented with respect.

I'll share with you one method I used that worked pretty well. About twenty-five years ago I was reading the book *Walden Pond* by Henry David Thoreau. In that book he writes, "If one advances confidently in the direction of his dreams, and endeavours to live the life which he has imagined, he will meet with a success unexpected in common hours."

I was unemployed at the time. My father had passed away a few months before, and I knew it was time for me to get on with my life. I knew I wanted to start a consulting company: I had some familiarity with business life and a reasonable amount of academic bench strength. I wanted a good living and to be my own boss.

As I sat in my apartment reading Thoreau's lines, I decided to put them to the test. I brought to mind an image that, for me, represented the busy consultant: I pictured myself, a file folder under my arm, walking very quickly to grab a ringing phone. The feelings the picture evoked were those of a successful, busy guy with things to do, responsibilities to fulfill, places to go.

I closed my eyes in a comfy chair in my living room. For about twenty minutes I visualized as many angles of this picture as I could. I held my attention as much as possible on the image and the feelings it evoked.

Because of Thoreau's guideline of endeavoring to live the life that I imagined, I very deliberately opened my eyes and declared, "Okay. I am now a consultant." It actually felt pretty good.

The next morning I was still in that frame of mind. "How powerful!" I thought. "I really am a consultant."

It was about 11 a.m. I was sitting in my comfy chair, unshaven, in my bathrobe, smoking a cigarette, glancing at the phone, and thinking, "Hmmm. The phone's not ringing."

That's when I realized that goals alone don't cut it. One needs the will to act. We'll get to that in the next couple of chapters. What I had managed to accomplish, however, was to get my goals into my unconscious mind. And that's our point.

When your goals are there, clear as day, embraced because they are intimately held and meaningful, then you're ready for operating, beyond ego, with others.

But your goals are only the first half of the equation. The goals of the people on your team are the other half.

UNCOVERING THE AUTHENTIC GOALS OF THE EMPLOYEE

What we must consider now is how you, as an influential leader, operating on automatic pilot, interact with your people in a way that moves them toward the team's goals.

The first thing you must do is know your people. So, at some point, perhaps during an annual review, or a scheduled coaching conversation, or even just tomorrow, you need to ask some very simple questions, and then listen for all you're worth. Predictably, the questions are:

- What are your goals?
- Why are these your goals?
- What steps are you planning to take to attain these goals?

But that's the easy part. Drilling deeper is the hard part. We need to get to their *real* goals. Too often people will tell their boss what the boss wants to hear.

Try it. Think of someone on your team who is engaged in some company-assigned task or mission or project. Ask them what their goals are for the project. The odds are very high they'll tell you that they are aiming to achieve the agreed-upon target. For example, if they are cleaning cafeteria trays, they might give the company line: "to clean all these trays without the conveyer belt jamming up." If you plead with them to give you an even more direct, or dare I say, honest, answer, they'll more likely say something like, "to go home early."

I thought about this phenomenon last week when I was doing a speaking engagement for a sales force. I was positive that if I were to approach any of the attendees and ask, "What's your goal?" one hundred percent of them would have clearly, loudly, and confidently answered, "To increase profitable volume by twenty percent over the next quarter versus last year."

I knew in my heart, however, having seen the spirit of authenticity drained from those conditioned soldiers of selling, that their real answer would have been — whispered, perhaps — to relax or to get promoted or to get out of sales or to get a new job or to make my target so I can make my bonus.

The point here is that being an influential leader means not hammering home the corporate mission unless it touches the aspirations, cravings, or needs of your people. If it doesn't, it will fall on deaf ears.

But why is it so difficult for managers to interact with their employees in this way?

Two Misperceptions

There are two main misperceptions that can hold you back from exploring and caring about an employee's goals before linking those goals to your goals or those of your organization.

Personal Goals Don't Belong

One misperception is that the employee's personal goals are not really relevant to you or the organization. You may find yourself thinking: "They're here to work. It's not my job to handhold them and listen to their personal concerns. Personal concerns are just that — personal."

You may believe that asking an employee about their goals is something to be dispensed with as quickly as possible so you can get on with what *really* matters: *your* goals for the employee, in light of the company's goals. This means you are being insincere when you ask for personal goals. Any employee can sniff that out with the ease of a bloodhound.

If this is your M.O., you will miss out on the deeper and more joyful side of working with people. The problem is that you want to get to dessert as quickly as possible, instead of enjoying it as the logical culmination of several courses of culinary delights. "Yes, yes, very nice; let's get down to business."

Confusing the personal with the private

The second misperception is closely related: confusing the personal with the private.

It's true that managing should not deal with private matters.

That *would* be inappropriate. But "personal" is not the same as "private." As an effective leader, you must ask about *personal* goals: what a person wants to get out of life, in a general sense; why they are working in this organization; where they see themselves going; what could be better for them in their work situation. Yes, you can even get into how the person is doing these days, so long as it's not perceived to be an invasion or doesn't become unduly time-consuming.

THE HARD PART OF LEADERSHIP

Once you have a close enough relationship with your people, it is time for you to practice what I think is the ultimate leadership skill of all: carving out your sentences so that you're speaking about what the organization needs done at the same time that you're addressing the true cravings of the employee. It's not so easy.

For example, let's say you manage a group of sales managers. Your goal for one of those managers is to get his team to produce at the same rate as that of his peers by the end of the next quarter. Uppermost in his mind, however, may be his need to finish building a deck in his backyard, or get his wife to find a new job, or put a stop to a lawsuit that's being pursued by a former employee.

He is not really interested in your goals until he feels at least heard concerning what he craves right now. And there's something even better than feeling heard: being assisted with his goal attainment. Ideally, you need to link what you want from him with what he wants.

That's the hard part. Connecting seemingly disparate goals so that both you and the employee are satisfied.

If he hits his quarter, will you help him build his deck? Will you help his wife find new work? Will you take over handling the lawsuit?

This may look too much like reciprocity. Or, perhaps you're thinking, "It's not appropriate to make deals like that because, for one thing, I don't have the time or resources to fulfill those promises."

No problem. The real challenge for the egoless leader is to rise above the seemingly no-win scenario and visualize a solution for all. In this game, egolessness is the key. It's hard for the ego to visualize win/win solutions. The ego is the one that thinks, "I don't wanna build a deck." "Why should I have to find his wife a job?" "I hate lawsuits."

Indeed, creativity is called for to find a single solution to two seemingly diverse challenges. And creativity is more likely to come from Self 2 than from Self 1. But just to be clear about this, if you can't find a creative solution, then actually "book off" a Saturday and give the guy a hand! In a very real, human way, you are, after all, two equals. You're in this together.

Okay. Even with that encouragement you don't want to help build a deck. Personally, I might just do it. But I get that you might not. And you're still not comfortable with finding a creative solution either. Perhaps you could just invest some time in regularly discussing his progress on the deck. Share in some of the slings and arrows of home construction. Even that genuine gesture alone would get you partway to making a connection with your employee.

But, in honor of the deck problem, and all the other employee personal cravings that I'm saying have to addressed in order to move employees toward your goals, let's at least look at what it means to be creative in this context. The ability to link what you want to what the employee craves is, after all, germane to your mission.

I used the words "rise above" a few paragraphs ago to point to the fact that sometimes a bird's eye view of a situation yields just the right vantage point to see an answer. Of course, it's just a metaphor; you can't really float up into the sky to see solutions. But I think there is an equivalent.

And we're not talking about compromise. That is, we're not saying you need to give a bit in order to gain a bit. You really shouldn't have to give up your Saturday in exchange for getting someone to buy into your goals.

I'm more interested in the more efficient, higher-level synthesis of your goal and the employee goal. The ideal is one gesture that gets at both missions. It's like you calling a customer in the building business and selling goods at cost in exchange for that customer selling your employee materials for his deck at cost. Everybody's a winner.

Let's stay longer with the deck example. How about paying for the deck in advance with the bonus money he will receive? There is evidence in the world of psychological research that you'll get even more commitment from the man when you offer this kind of gesture.

How about the whole sales team has a deck-building party? How about giving the employee extra time off when the quota has been reached so he can make a more focused building effort?

Or, break out of the box! Remember his other complaints? How about you just help his wife get a new job and forget about the deck? How about buying some time for your friend by having the legal department push the lawsuit back?

The idea is that he's your team member. He's got things on his mind. Address them with him. Make him feel your tangible, genuine support. Get him to embrace your goals for him while you embrace his. This is the stuff of humanity.

I get that your self-talk may be saying the equivalent of "no way." And if it is, then, well, I say back, "yes, way." But to digress for a moment, if that is what's going on for you, see how your self-talk is protecting you? See how you have certain beliefs and are using those beliefs to interpret these words and you are interpreting them in a way that supports those beliefs? Fascinating, isn't it?

Anyway, I *am* suggesting you get personal. And I am very confident things can work this way. Try it on for size. It doesn't have to absorb time. It's about human relationships. Until we die, we're involved in them.

The key is to rise above the normal dynamic and get personal. But how do you do that?

We'll talk about this more in later chapters, but for now let's just say that the ability to see the link between what the employee wants and what you want concerning that employee depends on whether you can shift perspectives or "see" things from a different vantage point. It's like you have to reorient yourself from your goal to the conjoining of the goals of the two parties involved.

It can be as simple as redirecting your attention by asking yourself a different question: instead of answering the question, "What do I need this person to do differently?" ask yourself, "What is the relationship between what I want this person to do differently and what this person wants?"

I refer to this as "rising above" because it is more of a macro perspective than a micro one, more global than local. You need to get a bird's-eye perspective rather than a ground-level one.

THE PARADOX OF PRESENCE

Paradoxically, leaders are most present in a conversation when they rise above the interaction itself. This sounds a little strange — as if the leader should somehow not be involved in the conversation, which could lead to some pretty strange meetings. However, we're talking about your doing these three things:

- Disengaging ego: letting go of the need to control, to win, or to be right
- Feeling empathy: seeing and embracing the point of view of the employee

- Being present: rising above the solo point of view of ego and adopting a vantage point that conjoins their goals and your goals

In your work as a leader, you must constantly create the opportunity to explicitly draw the link between your and your employee's goals. Aligning goals goes beyond sharing aspirations to reach a meeting of the minds on short-term and long-term goals and action steps for implementation.

Make sure you know your people well enough to understand their actual cravings on the job and maybe in life generally. And, when you are assigning a task, try your best to link the assignment to what's on the person's mind.

A big mistake leaders make is to say the equivalent of "This is what the company needs you to do," and, sometimes, "here's why." What they would be smarter to do is very explicitly link all of that to things like the person's interests, career goals, and fears.

To make this clear, have a look at the two trees in the diagram below.

Employee　　　　　　　　**Organization**

Think of a person's goals as the above-ground part of a tree. All the branches of the tree represent the goals of the diverse areas of that person's life. The smaller branches may be goals for various initiatives being undertaken (finish the deck, resolve the legal problem). The larger branches are the areas that those smaller branches belong to (make the home comfortable, keep business administrative matters running smoothly). But all the goals and categories of goals link to one thing: the trunk. The trunk represents that main aspiration in all of us: to feel whole or unified.

Companies work the same way. All activities can be traced to one main trunk, perhaps shareholder value or earnings. Out of that singular mission sprout multiple departments, initiatives, functions.

Now let me describe the big mistake that's often made using the metaphor of the tree described above. Leaders often link one assignment of the company, the tip of one twig in the tree, to the tip of one twig in the employee's tree. And they assume, "Good. Mission assigned and embraced."

But it doesn't really work that way. Or at least it's not nearly as motivating as when the leader traces, in the company's tree, the twig being assigned, its connection to the branch, and its connection to the main limb, and even that limb's connection to the trunk, and shows how the twig can be seen, upon being assigned to the employee's tree, to be traceable right down to the employee's trunk.

That's motivation.

For example, you are assigning to a person a critical-cost-analysis project that will directly affect profitability in your organization. People will be a little paranoid about the results of the analysis because it could mean fewer resources available to them. In addition to describing these facts, while you engage in a two-way discussion about the project, you say:

Consider this assignment a huge opportunity to gain greater visibility in the organization. That, of course, is right in line with what we talked about last week in terms of your career goals. You'll have to keep everyone fully informed of the progress you are making and you'll have to manage people's expectations. It's going to stretch your communication skills because you'll need a lot of finesse as you handle people's reactions. But that's okay because it's perfectly lined up with what we agreed last week about your development opportunities. So it's right up your alley. Let's figure out a schedule for us to touch base with each other on how it's going.

This principle of highlighting the links between employee needs and cravings and company and task goals is as simple as forming a sentence that explicitly draws the link between the company's goals and the employee's goals.

- Given that you want _____ and we need _____ how about we _____?
- How about you do _____? This gives you what you need but also satisfies the company's needs
- We have to find a way to _____ and still _____. At the same time we need to avoid _____.

Or, to fill in the blanks:

- Given that you want to get out of the office more, and we need to get more connected to our customers, how about we arrange a certain number of hours per week for you to be on the road?
- How about you do the reductions? This gives you some degree of control but also satisfies the company's needs to cut costs
- We have to find a way to increase morale and still remain within budget. At the same time we need to avoid the appearance of giving special treatment to the loudest voices

You should give the employee an opportunity to respond to the solution in order to set them up for authentic accountability and commitment to the aligned goal. You can ask questions to help draw this out.

- How do you feel about that?
- Can you implement that comfortably?
- Does that plan work for you?
- Do you see any possible issues with that?

Where there is concern, highlight the importance of the solution to achievement of their goals.

- In order to achieve your goal, it's important that we agree to a solution
- Committing to this solution will be an important step in achieving your goals

Finally, reinforce that commitment to the solution and specify an action plan that will play an important role in the achievement of their goals.

- By committing to this action plan, you are well on your way to achieving your goal of _____.
- If you can achieve this plan, then I'm confident that your goal of _____ will be met

Your words are powerful! The ones you choose will have a significant impact on your employee's commitment to their personal growth. The result of explicitly blending their goals with yours in conversation is an increase in their commitment level.

Smart leaders do this not only when they are one-on-one with their people, but in groups too. They do it when they assemble their team and make some stage-setting remarks about some matter.

Offering Your Perspective to the Group

In fact, one of the keys to being a good leader is helping your employees own, and be reminded of, a sense of vision. Without it, your team will likely wander off track. With a clear vision they will stay on track.

Vision is an interesting term when thought about in the context of self-talk or chatter. The leader's job is to be intimately involved in developing a vision, communicating it, and reminding people of it. A team's vision can become a predominant part of its members' self-talk. The team's vision makes for better self-talk than team members' private, sometimes negative chatter.

Vision is meant to replace self-talk. If the troops are troubled by insecurity, we need to replace that self-talk with a more desirable kind. I have heard more than one successful leader stand in front of his team and announce something like the following:

> The fact is that I don't know exactly how the organization is going to tackle this monster. We all know we have a problem here. And I'm confident that we'll solve it. I have no idea how. But I'm not going to let that into my thinking. I'm going to choose to focus on the job. I sincerely want you do the same. As tempting as it is, try not to get involved in worrying about it. You know your job well. Everybody in this room knows his or her job well. Whether this matter gets resolved or not does not affect our day-to-day jobs. I'd like you try to place your attention on the job. Face this challenge by gritting your teeth and doing as well as you can to satisfy our customers. Let's not lose track of what we do for a living around here.

This leader has attempted to replace his team's self-talk with a different one. He's trying to shift their focus. He has embraced not knowing the solution to the big problem and shown them a way out. This is leadership. We show them how to see the world. Otherwise, their own view just won't satisfy us.

There are some handy ingredients to include when you prepare group remarks of this nature. Following this recipe can get you started. The key is to blend together the thoughts, feelings, and perspectives of your team members while you give them something to aspire to.

1. Context-setting remark — so they know what you're talking about
2. Empathy for what they are feeling — so they feel heard and understood by you
3. A clear statement of how you want them to interpret the matter at hand — so they know what you expect of them. This statement needs to show how the desired interpretation is better than the present interpretations
4. Confidence in their ability to fulfill this vision of yours — so they have self-confidence
5. Comment about the obstacles they will face as they attempt to implement the vision — so they won't be surprised when things don't go perfectly

Having made ground in the previous chapter on demonstrating empathy, and in this one on aligning employees' goals with your own, you are ready for the last two chapters in this part of the book, on supporting self-esteem and inspiring commitment. Read on.

■

CHAPTER SEVEN

Drawing on the
Source of Engagement

Let's talk about self-esteem. First, we'll define it and compare it with ego so there is no confusion. Second, we will explore how your ego can get engaged situationally, and how self-esteem is what can loosen the shackles of that engagement. Third, we'll consider one example each of low and high self-esteem at work and show the link between high self-esteem and employee engagement. Finally, with that link in mind, we'll consider how you can foster the self-esteem of the people on your team.

SELF-ESTEEM AND EGO

Many people think that high self-esteem equates to a healthy ego. But that depends on how you use the terms. Remember, the definition of ego that we're using says it's the part of you that sees yourself as above, below, or against other people or circumstances. From that point of view, you are essentially in a challenging place, experiencing one or more of the following: lamenting an inferior position; feeling the need to highlight or retain a superior position; laboring emotionally over an obstacle or challenge. If you are a person with an egocentric vantage point, you are constantly wrestling with how you are doing personally versus how you want things to be.

Self-esteem is very different. Self-esteem is what you bring with you to that vantage point. High self-esteem equates to your faith that you will handle whatever unfolds (you are *able*) and that, at the core, you are okay (you are *valuable*).

Picture this. You are visiting the old homestead. In the morning you announce to those around you, "When breakfast is over, I'm going to hop in the car and drive to the store."

Your great-great-grandmother is sitting there, drinking some hot water with lemon. "Oh, no, dear," she says to you. "That's too dangerous. It's bad out there. Speeders. People slamming on their brakes. Not using turn signals. Cutting you off."

You smile and feel love as you reply, "It's okay, Granny, I'll be fine."

That's the first half of self-esteem. Indeed, there likely will be some challenges on the road, but you know that you're quite capable of handling them.

But great-great-grandpa is there too and he mumbles just under his breath: "You're a worthless piece of junk."

That one goes in one ear and out the other. His aspersion pushes no buttons. You spend no time on it because you know your inherent value. There is no question. At least in *your* mind, anyway.

That's the other half of self-esteem. You experience yourself as inherently valuable.

However, while self-esteem is the faith that you are able and the experience of being of value, ego is the part of you that has its doubts about that or something to prove about that.

Situational egocentricity

The vast majority of people are not egocentric all the time. Indeed, certain things trigger certain people. You may be externally focused on some tasks and suddenly, with the right provocation, become quite egocentric. Perhaps on a blue day your great-great-grandpa's judgment may have set off a deep-seated fear of being unloved. Perhaps, the week after you were involved in a car accident, your great-great-grandma's fear may have kept you from leaving the house. We all rise and fall.

Similarly, there can be fluctuations in a person's level of self-esteem.

I like to see self-esteem and ego as two different dimensions against which a person can be measured. At any given point, a person can be highly egocentric or not engaged at all, or can have high self-esteem or low self-esteem. These two dimensions can be compared using a two-by-two matrix, such as in the diagram below.

High Ego Engagement

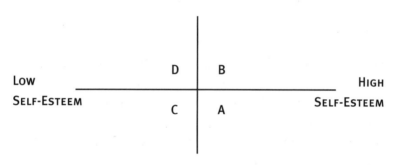

Low Ego Engagement

In the lower right quadrant (A) is someone whose ego is not engaged and who has high self-esteem. This may be a leader on the job who is succeeding at getting her team engaged and whose attention is on making things happen. It's not about her; it's about the mission.

In the upper right quadrant (B) is the person whose ego is engaged and who has high self-esteem. This state of mind means that the person sees himself as above, below, or up against someone or some circumstance but because of high self-esteem is able to self-manage effectively. For example, think of someone who is working hard to get a promotion. During the interview, directing her attention to herself is fairly desirable. Her ego feels engaged but she is psychologically well equipped to handle the circumstance.

In the bottom left quadrant (C) is someone with low self-esteem and low ego engagement. An example of this frame of mind is someone who doesn't have faith in himself but who is not presently preoccupied with his circumstances or with comparing himself with others.

Finally, in the upper left quadrant (D) is a person who is highly egocentric at the moment and with low self-esteem. This is a person who would find it difficult to switch gears or self-manage.

Your challenge as a leader is to take your high self-esteem to the non-ego vantage point.

It isn't always easy. Throughout this book we've been discussing how your self-talk chatters away, often revealing your egocentric stance. It's making its judgments and reaching its opinions with a certain circularity that reinforces your beliefs, relative to your position in the world. Rather than addressing the object-level world — the world of objects and real events — it is playing at the meta level, deciding for itself whether things are the way they ought to be.

Through self-management, however, you can catch yourself judging and recognize how you are only reinforcing your prejudices. You can set the self-talk aside and genuinely listen to another person's point of view. You can use your insight into the person's cravings and needs in order to visualize the relationship between what you want from that person and what they want from you. Your self-esteem gives you the will to self-manage, and with practice, to do so more and more consistently.

Choices

When you have high self-esteem, you are able to operate independently of fears, of deeply rooted, twisted needs to achieve at all costs, and of an interest in appearing to others to be superior. High self-esteem means the doorways to personal passion and joy on the job are wide open. In fact, the essence of engagement for people is passion flowing from the unfolding of their unique, inherent individuality. That's quite different from passion that flows because leaders have deliberately or unwittingly stirred up egos. This latter type of passion is usually short-lived. It is dependent on constant stirring from the outside (threats, compensation plans, promises). What we're interested in is passion that is not imposed, but self-initiated.

Overriding robotic responses and ego

The ability to choose does not just involve the choices you make on the job, such as to phone that supplier right now, to address certain problems at 2 p.m., to get the agenda ready for the weekly meeting. It also involves the choice to override your habitual, robotic responses — and your ego as a whole. For example, when you have high self-esteem and somebody is nasty to you, you are more resilient. While you may feel the impulse to take something personally, you choose to let it go.

Curiously enough, getting into the habit of overriding impulses is the path to more self-esteem. When you have high self-esteem you are able to override impulses. And, to elevate your level of self-esteem, you can practice overriding impulses. It works both ways.

It was a somewhat sad day for me about fifteen years ago to conclude from a book I was reading (*The Road Less Traveled* by M. Scott Peck) that a greater degree of mental health can be achieved by doing little things that you don't want to do. Now that was just downright bad news. I was a private hedonist, accustomed to spoiling myself with the pleasures of life. The last thing a hedonist wants to hear is that immersing yourself in the pleasures of life is actually bad for you.

As I was embracing that possibility, I was speaking to a colleague of mine about a conflict I was experiencing in my life. For fifteen or so years I had been standing in front of audiences declaring with full confidence, "You can choose to be happy!" After such presentations, I would get into my car, or go back to my hotel room, and mutter under my breath, "Nah, I don't buy that." I explained to my friend that I was saying something I didn't really believe. (This is commonly referred to as lying — though I preferred spinning it as experiencing cognitive dissonance.)

My doubts about picking myself up by my own bootstraps came from the fact that my own self-esteem was not in great shape.

My friend gave me good advice. He pointed out that getting to my next meeting involved using the subway system. "When you get off the subway car at the target station, you are confronted with the ultimate existential choice — taking the stairs or the escalator."

"Yes," I replied hesitantly.

"Take the stairs."

It was another shot of bad news. My friend was agreeing with the book about the advantages of impulse management. He was recommending that I do the thing I least wanted to do: take the stairs less traveled.

The good news is that it works. If you want a piece of apple pie, wait fifteen minutes. If you don't want to clean the yard because you're feeling lazy, do it anyway. If you don't want to get to that spreadsheet, now's the time. These impulses to be lazy come from ego. They represent you against the world. "I want my pie now." Overriding these impulses will strengthen your ability to lift yourself out of a robotic war with the world.

For the last five years or so I have been doing aerobic exercises pretty much every day. It's a habit now, but some days are harder than others. I often wonder where the will to work out comes from. I know it's from me, but where did I get it? My best friend says it's a fear of death. My own view is that if that's true, the ability to overcome the fear is at least supplemented by practiced impulse management.

So if you want to improve your self-esteem, one thing you can do is practice making little choices that involve overriding little preferences. Don't try to do something too big. That will just disappoint you and cause you to discontinue the exercise.

Self-esteem does not come just from our own efforts, however. There is no doubt that it can be traced back to childhood. That's where we first learn whether we are okay or not. When a child knows she's okay in her parents' book, no matter what, she takes criticism and hears the inevitable periodic anger toward her in that context. She knows that she's okay but this particular behavior is not.

Self-esteem will change, however, over the span of your life. A bad boss can drag it down. Professional success can raise it up. Your home life, with all its joys and challenges, will have an impact on it. The economy, social change, political evolution, changes at work, health matters can all affect it. The more self-esteem you start with, and the more self-esteem you hold on to, and the more you nurture it, the better off you are.

LOW AND HIGH SELF-ESTEEM ON THE JOB

Let's look at some examples of self-esteem in the workplace.

Low self-esteem

I coached a young executive who worked in a corporation that sent new hires to executive coaches to help them make the transition to their new responsibilities effectively. This fellow, we'll call him Robert, was very open to being coached. He was eager to be successful in his new job. He shared with me some 360° reports he had received during his career. And he invited me to speak

discreetly with some of his new peers. I also had a one-hour interview with Robert's boss.

Robert was seen by his new peer group as smart, but somewhat politically naive. They thought he talked too much and he
got kind of loud when he got excited. One of his colleagues whispered to me that she thought he was "full of himself."

I couldn't help notice that Robert was very proud of his new
role. He had bought a whole new wardrobe and, as part of his
compensation plan, had leased a particularly splashy corporate
car and joined an expensive golf club. "You have to look the part,
you know what I mean?" he said to me in our first meeting, smil-
ing. I did know what he meant.

Robert's 360° reports were pretty interesting, particularly the
feedback from some of his former employees. Some commented
that he could be a bit of a bulldog. When he wanted something,
he wouldn't let go. They also indicated that Robert could get
pretty aggressive when he was frustrated and so could be difficult
to be around.

Robert described himself as a workaholic. That, along with his
tenacity, was what he believed got him to where he was in his career.

How does Robert look to you? Does he appear to be a normal
young executive with a few rough edges? That's pretty much
how I see him. To get to positions like his, in an organization like
his, does take a certain kind of powerful personality, a certain
kind of pride in image. It was clear to me that his rough edges
related to ego, but as his coach it was not my job to take him
apart and criticize self-centeredness unless there was an issue
that he needed to get his head around.

Robert was not asking me to facilitate his growth in any deep
way. If he had, we would have focused on why he wanted to be
seen in a certain light (clothes, golf membership, car), and why
he was like a bulldog, and what beliefs about himself were underneath his periodic aggression, and what was behind his worka-

holism. Indeed, I might have been inclined to facilitate self-discovery regarding his ego. And I might have helped him see that his self-esteem was low and that he was okay in my books whether he had this job or any other job.

Instead of exploring these heavier things, we looked at how he could be more graceful in his communications, both with his peers and with his boss.

However, I did have the occasion to ask him a question that turned out to be productive.

"Do you feel that you are okay, regardless of how you perform in your job?"

"What do you mean?" he replied.

"Well, I'm wondering about the extent to which you define yourself by how well you do at work. I get the feeling that, in a sense, you *are* your work, such that if your work fails, then *you* would be a failure. That actually happens to be why I think you work so hard. You have a lot of skin in the game."

"I know what you mean," he replied. He paused for a moment, then said, "Now *that's* provocative." He took another moment. Then, smart fellow that he was, he said, "Well now, that's a bit of a no-win scenario isn't it?"

I nodded.

"How could someone step out of that paradigm?" I asked.

Then we talked about self-esteem.

Of course, you can't just tell someone these things and have them simply switch gears. It doesn't work that way. Even though with high self-esteem one can indeed pick oneself up by one's own bootstraps, there are some practical limits involved. But to confront the fact that much of what you do may be coming from an egocentric place and to consider the possibility of finding a healthier frame of mind can set one on a new course that over a lifetime can lead to greater peace and more opportunities for flowing in the moment.

Interestingly, even the relatively profound questioning of one's egocentricity may itself be a matter of ego. After all, when Robert wonders about whether he is egocentric, he is inquiring of himself whether he is possibly "below" some better place of being. But that's okay. That's what picking oneself up by one's own bootstraps is all about. Over time Robert may catch his egocentricity while in the act and his experience with reflecting on his patterns may give him the boost he needs to climb out.

One of the questions Robert asked me was whether a person can have too much self-esteem. What do you think?

When people have healthy self-esteem, their attention is usually not on themselves; it is external to themselves. They have a high degree of faith in their ability to deal with their world and in their inherent value. So they are not the star of the show. What's going on around them is the star of the show.

In contrast, somebody who is, as Robert was alleged to be, "full of himself" has his attention tightly focused on himself: demonstrating *his* ability and *his* value. So no, I don't subscribe to the notion that it's possible to have too much self-esteem. My experience is that when someone projects a high level of self-esteem, they want you to perceive them that way. That's ego. It's about them.

High self-esteem

Now let's look at a case of what I would call very healthy self-esteem. I worked with a man who is the senior vice president of sales and marketing for a large, global pharmaceutical company. Let's call him Jeremy.

Jeremy is a highly respected leader. He appears neither arrogant nor humble. He is focused on the job. People feel that he hears them. He addresses their needs. He *did* help one of his regional leaders build a deck in his backyard. He doesn't talk about himself much. But he'll talk about you.

I asked him once to tell me about himself and he answered with nothing but the basics. And his answer was brief. He quickly steered his answer to a description of his family.

I offered that his answer seemed humble.

"I'm nothing special and not worthy of great discussion. I love what I do. I facilitate others to reach goals. And together we achieve big goals as a world-class corporation that brings greater health to humanity. What better job could there be?"

"Do you like how far you've come in your career?"

"I don't think about it."

"Oh, come on. You must have some pride in your achievements."

"Look. I just don't go there. We can talk about me if you want but not about how proud I am of myself. That just seems juvenile. Sure, I've made progress. There has been a lot of hard work and a lot of support from some very dedicated and smart people."

"Okay, let's not talk about you then," I said. "Tell me about some of the challenges you face these days on the job."

His answers were fascinating. They contained facts about the competition, regulatory changes, hierarchical bureaucracy, and the educated consumer. Asked to explain why these were challenges, he stuck with the facts. He didn't blame anybody. He saw things for what they were. I asked about politics at the office and he had no comments. He wasn't resisting the discussion, he just said, "I don't think about it."

"Do you ever lose your temper?"

"Rarely, at least not in front of anybody — that would be undesirable," he said.

"Are you passionate about your work?"

"Absolutely. We have tough goals and I love the quest."

"So there's room for passion but none for frustration? It sounds a little out of balance. Doesn't one go with the other?"

"Loving what you do might set you up for frustration when

things don't go well. But the question is what you do with that frustration. You can lament the facts around you or you can address them."

You may think this man can afford to act this way, given his position, his likely income, and the amount of respect he gets from others. But it's all relative, if you know what I mean. For example, he reports to a COO, who in turn reports to a CEO, who reports to a board. Jeremy has never met the chair of the board. I'm more inclined to say that his success correlates to his healthy self-esteem rather than that the self-esteem comes from his role.

FOSTERING SELF-ESTEEM IN YOUR EMPLOYEES

I hope by now that it makes perfect sense to you that your job is to support the self-esteem of the people on your team. Doing so is more likely to elevate their sense of will, to facilitate their sense of engagement, to reinforce their willingness to make difficult choices. We'll see in the next chapter that it elevates their capacity to commit and live by their word. But how do we grant this gift?

There are both subtle and obvious ways for you to support self-esteem.

Subtle ways to support self-esteem

The key is to come to the task from a place of low ego. This helps you avoid being a big contributor to the egocentric fears and games of your team members. You will need to have some grip on your self-talk habits. You will need to catch yourself before you make personal judgments. You will need to disengage your self-talk while you listen to others, so that they will feel heard. You will need to be sufficiently other-oriented to find it within yourself to care about their goals and be skilled at weaving together the ingredients of their goal fulfillment and the organization's goal attainment.

Basically, you will need to catch yourself making things about you, and to shift gears into making them about the mission or task at hand.

The secret to building the self-esteem of others is helping them realize that they are not doomed by your judgments. They need to know that their making mistakes is okay with you. You may evaluate their behavior on the job, but you will not evaluate who they are. And don't just rely on their figuring this out for themselves over time. Why not make it clear?

There's nothing wrong with telling someone some version of what you, I hope, were told as a kid: "I love you, but I don't always love the things you do." In the workplace it could go like this: "You know, you're okay in my books. I promise that I will not judge you. You will undoubtedly find me assessing the things you do, and you don't have to worry about my extending that to who you are. The fact that you are here means you've already passed the test. You're in the club. You'll always stay in the club of people I will be there for."

The field of psychotherapy calls this approach "unconditional positive regard." Originally expressed by Carl Rogers, known by some to be the founder of client-centered therapy and perhaps a co-founder of humanism itself, the phrase is meant to say, "No matter what, you're okay." This, as we said, is one of the two core beliefs that correlate to high self-esteem. The idea here is that as a leader you may as well demonstrate it and specify it.

You may feel that this is going too far. "Yes, but what if you say that to someone and ultimately have to fire them?" you may be thinking. My response is that the behavior on the job is very distinct from your unconditional positive regard of their individual humanity. Surely even the people you dismiss from your organization are still worthy of your support.

This takes us to a particularly subtle notion to wrestle with for a moment. Being beyond ego implies that you no longer see things as polarities: good or bad, right or wrong, either one thing or another. As my friend John said just the other day in an email to me, "It's all in the 'and.'" By that he was rejecting that something is either right or wrong. That thing is what it is. Instead, let's ask what this thing helps us learn and what it leads to?

For example, when Mary is consistently late, it's helpful to keep in mind that life is busy. Sometimes work, for Mary, is a drag. Not everyone gets to live close to the office. Whatever stuff Mary hides or uses to explain the incessant tardiness has got be compassionately understood by you. Yes, being late has negative consequences. But let's not forget that from Mary's perspective, getting there on time may be a real drag. Both perspectives are true. Don't judge Mary. Rise above the notion that somebody is right or wrong and find a solution.

You and Mary have an awful lot in common. For example, at the risk of being melodramatic, you are both going to die someday. You will both scan back and assess how you did during your time on the planet. Her lateness will not reflect unfavorably on her. Let's keep it in perspective. Fix the problem. Love the person.

You build self-esteem in others when they see that you get it. You've got a vision. You will reach the vision. And you get what they're wrestling with. You'll help them as much as you can. And you'll both reach the vision together.

Obvious ways to support self-esteem

It's no surprise that a great tool for supporting self-esteem is in giving someone a compliment. After all, it recognizes a person favorably and so directly touches their sense of being able and valuable.

I'm a believer in giving lots of compliments, as long as they are genuine. For some people it can take a lot of mental effort to think of honest, nice things to say to employees. Sometimes the employees don't appear to do anything special and sometimes the boss is too negatively judgmental to have any positive thoughts available. This book has already addressed the latter matter.

Regarding the suggestion that the employee does nothing special, I don't buy it. They show up for work. That is an exercise of their will. They lift their hand. That shows positive intention to act. They ask questions and that shows curiosity. They argue back, and that shows investment in our success. They make mistakes, so they're trying. The idea is that if you see things without an ego posture, then there's a positive side to most things. Your job is to touch their spirit with your recognition of that positive side.

One thing I try to do with people when I give them feedback is be very specific. I try to highlight a choice the person made and the consequence of that choice. Rather than saying, "Bill, way to go at the meeting this morning; you da man," I say something like: "Bill, when you heard Roger make his point at the meeting this morning, I saw you glance over at Lucille. Then you chose to speak up to support Roger's position. That led to positive discussion and eventual resolution of Roger's issue. Good choice."

The same thing goes for constructive feedback. Be specific and talk about consequences. For example, rather than: "Ricardo, you submitted the spreadsheet without checking it again. You've got to check the spreadsheets!" try: "Ricardo, there were some slips in this week's spreadsheet. Remember our discussion about that? Anyway, when you were done with the entries, I think you just saved the file and sent it off. This meant a few of us had to catch inconsistencies and correct things for you. I suggest that next time, before you hit 'save,' stop yourself, check your entries, and then go for it."

In both the positive feedback and the negative feedback examples above, emphasis is placed on the choices employees made and on the consequences of those choices. This focus actually somewhat celebrates or honors the person's capacity to choose. Earlier we said that the things you do to elevate self-esteem (overriding little impulses) are the same behaviors that exhibit self-esteem (the capacity to override impulses). In this way, highlighting and honoring choices produces choices. That's what self-esteem is all about.

HEADING FOR COMMITMENT

In this part of this book, we have focused on how you as a leader interact with others. The building blocks we have examined are: demonstrating empathy; aligning goals with your employees as real, breathing human beings whose needs are as relevant to them as your goals are to you; and, in this chapter, supporting their self-esteem, the very source of engagement.

There's one more building block to examine — inspiring commitment — before moving to the third part of the book on big-picture thinking.

■

CHAPTER EIGHT

INSPIRING COMMITMENT

How can leaders develop employees who are truly committed to doing their jobs with excellence and driving results for the entire organization?

Given what we've been exploring together in this part of the book, you may be anticipating the answer to that question. The leaders who inspire commitment in their employees are ones who:

- Make sure their employees feel heard
- Align employee personal cravings and goals with managerial goals
- Support their employees' self-esteem
- Create a non-judgmental, non-blame-oriented environment where people feel free to take risks
- Live by their word and expect others to do the same
- Ask for commitment
- Do all these things through the grid of their own self-management

Since self-management is the key to it all, this chapter will certainly address your own skills and habits in this area. And, of course, we will also consider your task of inspiring commitment and developing a culture of accountability. But first we need to look at what "commitment" actually means and consider why so many of us are dysfunctional committers.

What Is Commitment?

True commitment involves the investment of one's whole being into what one says one will do. If a truly committed person says, "I will be there by 3 p.m.," then watch out! They don't utter the words lightly; there is a feeling a full intentionality behind them.

But it's not just at the moment they utter the words that they feel this intentionality. Commitment also means carrying or sustaining that sense of intentionality over the passage of time.

If you have children, the odds are that you have this sense of commitment toward them. You can look your son or daughter in the eye and with absolute certainty declare, "You can absolutely count on me." And you mean it, with all of your being. You live it. In some sense, you *are* your word.

For me, any commitment made to anyone requires this same sense of clarity, certainty, and conviction. You are your word.

This is why there is a strong relationship between self-esteem and commitment. When you have high self-esteem, you have a strong sense or feeling of who you are, a strong sense of self. There is a central you and you can feel it; you sense yourself as a whole individual — undivided by fear, self-doubt, and self-deception — capable of wholly committing to an outcome.

This central you is not your ego. Recall that ego is the part of you that sees itself as below, above, or up against other people and things. You can still experience a feeling of a central you with your ego disengaged. You are not your ego. For example, you can experience yourself as seamlessly connected with others, or one who sees that things are unfolding as they should, or one with the will to create new possibilities. Or all of these and more.

It's pretty interesting that we use the word "will" to describe the strength of our convictions or our willpower. When you have more will, you are more are able to get past obstacles, take on bigger challenges, move bigger mountains. When I tell my son, "I will be there for you, no matter what," I'm investing my whole being, with all of my strength, my willpower, in that commitment.

The fact that we use the word "will" to express our future intentions, as in "I will see you at 3," is also pretty interesting. When we talk about that word, we are talking about *being*. That notion can be hard to get a grip on, but for our purposes it's actually pretty straightforward.

In the present tense, we say "I am" when we refer to our being. "I am happy." "I am Arthur." These expressions are about *being* something. When we talk about our being in the future we say, "I will be," as in "I will be at the train station by noon." Think about that. We refer to our *being* when we commit. "I will be there for you" means you can absolutely count on me.

Commitment can be a most beautiful thing. So why is there not more of it? Why don't people make commitments? Why don't they follow through on their commitments? Why do they not take responsibility for failing to fulfill their commitments?

WHERE'S THE COMMITMENT?

There is no lack of people with some kind of commitment problem. Here are three common commitment dysfunctionalities:

1. *Fear of commitment.* Some people may have a fear of failure, fear of success, fear of rejection, fear of confrontation, fear of exposure, fear of disappointing others, even a fear of fear. It keeps them from making commitments

2. *Deflecting responsibility.* "It's not my fault" can be a subtle reflection of a discomfort with commitment or an initial lack of commitment. "Oops, honey, I was no longer driving in the direction of the dry cleaners so it simply no longer made sense"

3. *Committing in bad faith.* Many of us are muddled in our intentions and convictions. For example, we may have problems fulfilling our promises to ourselves about things like cigarette smoking, weight-

loss programs, exercise routines, extramarital affairs, alcohol con-
sumption. We can be tempted by our appetites (literally and figura-
tively) or even just plain forget our promises. Sometimes we over-
extend ourselves, making commitments we just cannot keep or
making them somewhat mindlessly

It's not that we're bad people. We're human. But, we can self-
manage! Let's look at these three commitment issues one at a
time to get a better idea of how commitment works and how we
can personally embrace it and cause it in others.

Fear of Commitment

Like many people, you may be afraid to commit. And your
employees may sense it.

Fear of commitment is often generated by the ego. When you
have the perspective of yourself as below others or up against big
challenges, it can be frightening to declare to the universe, "Here
I come!"

You may be like a young man I know who seemed to be hedg-
ing his bets by saying to the woman he loved, "Perhaps we should
set a time six months from now when we can decide when we're
going to get engaged." The woman suspected that if an engagement date actually emerged from this "engagement for an
engagement to get engaged," he would want the wedding to be
at least a year off, with the engagement and wedding date not
made public for another period of time.

What was happening here? This young man was setting up
escape routes all along his path. He was clearly protecting himself
from giving himself away — from being the "I am" who is the "I
will." In fact, because he couldn't say "I am" and "I will," he was
afraid to say, "I do."

I can identify with him. In my twenties, I had a hard time
committing to long-term relationships. I was probably terrified

of giving myself away only to be hurt. This was partly irrational, but also partly rational. After all, the statistic was in the news that 50% of marriages ended in divorce. That made it reasonable to avoid marriage: What kind of a lying fool would I be if I stood in front of others and promised this woman that I'd love her till death do us part, in the light of this plain, objective fact that when the honeymoon was over, the marriage might be over?

Finally, I got close. When I was in the best relationship I had ever experienced, I said to my friends, "This one is the one, for sure. As long as neither of us changes as people and as long as we're faithful to each other . . ."

A brutally honest friend saw through me with x-ray vision. "You still don't get it, do you?" he said. "You're giving yourself an out. You're setting conditions to your commitment."

I saw myself in that instant as standing on the diving board of life, unable to make the jump.

I suspect that marriages that begin with prenuptial agreements don't last as long. I know from experience that business commitments made with exit clauses often don't last long. They aren't true commitments. When your people hear you say, "We are *aiming* for a 20 percent increase," they can just intuit that you've built in an escape route. And you are setting a bad example.

Real commitment requires a certain kind of "no matter what" to it. It requires what some folks refer to as a "leap of faith." It's a jump out of the realm of figuring things out and into the realm of what will be. I am now committed to my wife for life. Period. You may present me with all the things that may go wrong, but I'm just not going to entertain them. As soon as we begin to visualize what might excuse us, we begin the process of letting ourselves off the hook.

Commitment is partly about getting past fear. It takes a faith in oneself. Sometimes "realists" have a challenge with commitment because they lack this faith. They are perhaps more inclined to enumerate all the things that work against the fulfillment of a promise. Think of a meeting room at your office with a group of salespeople sitting around the table. You, as the sales leader, are declaring, "We must exceed last year's volume by 25%." The people around the room respond with, "not in this economy," "look at the inflexibility of our pricing policies," "competition is cutthroat; it can't be done," "we don't have the administrative staff we need to be adequately focused on the marketplace." The list could go on.

What's wrong with considering the list of obstacles? Nothing. But eventually you have to move past that list and into the world of commitment. As the leader of that team you need to hear people out, address what can be addressed, but move the individuals on the team on to commitment based on their belief in themselves. Self-esteem is the primary ingredient to that personal commitment.

As the leader, you benefit highly from knowing that fear is an obstacle to commitment and that people use their view of reality to give a voice to their fears. And your job as a leader is to move people out of their fear space and into self-confidence. Deal with reality, for sure: it's what's flowing at you. Strategize. But do it in the context of confidence and not out of fear.

This is not to say that there is no limit to what you should commit to. Indeed, there is a huge role for realism. The key is to recognize when providing and analyzing a list of obstacles is actually coming from an ego expressing fear and thereby being an obstacle to personal expression and stretching.

This means you must be skilled at managing your own self-talk. You too must choose confidence. It's a leap.

DEFLECTING RESPONSIBILITY

For the same reason that people resist committing in order to avoid that shrinking feeling that comes from failure, many also often respond defensively to implications and accusations about culpability. Responsibility for failure is a soft spot for most people. It's why we resist taking that responsibility up front. It's why we deflect it after the damage is done.

We said that people sometimes use an analysis of reality to express their fears. Now let's look briefly at how they do that to explain their personal failures. In both cases, ego is engaged. When you're fearful, it's ego. When you defend against what went wrong, it's ego.

It can be interesting to observe different patterns in the way that people "attribute" misfortune. Some of us lean toward a natural and basic, "It's not my fault." Others habitually go so one step further and cite just whose fault it is. Some are inclined to look inward and feel shame. Others will experience that same sense of full responsibility but not have guilt. This last group is more likely to simply learn, and move into action.

My favorite term for a person with this healthy stance on life's challenges is "agent," as in "cause agent" or "agent of change." Agents possess "agency."

Agency is defined by Oxford as "action personified." It's the perfect term for depicting the tendency to move into action rather than spend time on blame. The agent is one who takes full responsibility, the committed player. The person who holds herself fully accountable yet won't be neurotic in reacting to failure, instead saying, "I own it; here's my plan."

Agents are distinct, then, from victims ("Oh, I've had such a hard shift so far"); deflectors ("My goodness, didn't Billie get to that? I told him about it an hour ago"); and personalizers ("I am just so awfully sorry for not having gotten to you before this").

Agency, thank goodness, can be adopted. You can learn to recognize victim-like self-talk in yourself, for example, and make an effort to self-correct. For example, instead of thinking or declaring, "It's those guys again," you might think or say, "I own it. I will figure this thing out."

Just to make this clear, you can actually catch yourself looking to attribute blame and before you say a deflecting word, connect with the willful override, "I own this."

COMMITTING IN BAD FAITH

You have probably heard the term "bad faith." It comes from the twentieth-century French existentialist philosopher Jean-Paul Sartre but has become well known outside the academic world. It refers to the lies we tell ourselves. Sartre says bad faith is a capacity built right into our way of being. It's not that we knowingly tell ourselves falsehoods. It's that we take a position on a matter even though some other part of us does not or cannot hold that position. Bad faith creates profound alienation from ourselves and therefore is another way we reveal that commitment is an issue.

Not dealing with an employee problem, knowing that you should do so, is bad faith. So is planning to get started on an exercise program but never getting around to it. In both of these examples there are at least two parts of you involved: the part that believes you should act and the part that doesn't want to.

The interesting thing about bad faith is that there is a certain game going on in your head. Your consciousness does not let the part that wants to act get wholly heard. Somehow you manage to hide from that desire. It only vaguely reaches the level of awareness and is then quickly submerged again with a, "Yes, I have to get to that," or "My goodness, I've really been procrastinating on that."

Sometimes people aren't really interested in the thing they are being asked to commit to. That can lead to bad faith. It happens when a leader does not tap into the employee's true cravings and fears. Ignoring these motivators and just laying out the mission is the perfect recipe to create bad faith among team members.

Sometimes bad faith sets in when our lives are going quickly and we promise things that just aren't going to happen. This is extraordinarily common.

I recall a striking example of this phenomenon. About fifteen years ago my firm got its first large client. We had previously served only relatively small businesses, so this big break meant an awful lot. The project was with a world-class organization with a world-recognized brand. It was very exciting and probably quite a milestone. We were basically told by other large organizations subsequent to getting this first monster client, "If you're good enough for them, I'm sure you'll be fine for us."

To get the project rolling, I was asked to speak to the executive VP of sales and marketing. This was a man six layers from the front lines. He was so high up, I didn't even know the organization had such a position. (So much for my ability to know my clients.) I was nervous. I thought, "Wow. This will be the first time I've ever actually met a god."

I was escorted into his mansion of an office and wasn't sure which seat to take. There was the living-room area over there, there was the boardroom table the size of my house over on that side, and there were a couple of visitor chairs in front of his expansive desk some distance up ahead. I just stood there, somewhat in awe, undoubtedly nervous, sort of waiting for things to evolve.

When god got off the phone he motioned me to the boardroom table. He took the head of the table, leaned way back, and began asking me questions. I think I did okay. Then he asked, "Do you have a copy of our financial statements?" I replied in the negative, and I was a little embarrassed. Then with a wave of his hand he said, "I'll get one sent to you."

I was struck by those words. I thought, "Now when somebody this big, this powerful says that he'll do something, I imagine that before I get back to my office, that darned thing will be done."

I did notice, however, that he didn't write it down. To that I thought, "Well, I imagine that when you're this big and powerful, you don't even need to take notes."

I've actually stopped waiting, but it's been fifteen years and the package still hasn't arrived. Processing things pretty quickly at the time, I concluded only a few weeks after that it wasn't likely to arrive. It has struck me ever since: the big guy said he would do something and it just didn't happen.

In his case I suppose that he was not mindful when he said what he was going to do that he actually made the "commitment." He certainly didn't know that he was talking to someone who was anal retentive enough to hold onto the problem for a decade or two.

I wonder whether his commitment came from Self 1 or Self 2? Let's think about this.

Self 2 is the automatic pilot. It's what's underneath self-talk. As we said earlier, we can operate pretty quickly from that level and get things right. The executive didn't seem egocentric when we interacted. I didn't feel that he had a need to impress, at least not in that conversation. It just seemed to happen.

I would wager that his commitment did come from Self 2. It wasn't his self-talk offering a commitment that he had no intention of fulfilling. The problem was that his Self 2 was not particularly skilful at catching the little promises he would make.

In other words, we're not concluding in this book that your Self 2 is enlightened! It is only as skilled or practiced as you have made it to be. If you have the habit of glibly making promises, then that's what is going to show up for others to see — ego or no ego.

Looking at this challenge for you as a leader, the idea is for you to slow things down when you start talking about what you'll do for someone. Mean the words. Let your self-talk catch you going too quickly (self-talk in its most productive form!). You can self-manage your way out of glibly offering what is unrealistic. You can self-manage yourself into slowing down, writing down your commitments, and acting on them later.

Let's collect our thoughts about bad faith. The moment after this man said he would do something, he let it go. He was in bad faith. He told himself a lie. In the earlier example of bad faith we said that when you get employees to commit to something that they don't buy into, you're creating an environment where bad faith can run rampant. They may procrastinate on some things and sabotage others. And they may not be fully aware of it. The same applies to you. When you know you've got an issue tucked away in some corner of your world, sitting there, and you know better, but you don't deal with it, you're in bad faith.

Once bad faith has set in, there are two ways to get real relief.

One is to actually act on whatever matter we're lying to ourselves about. For example, when you finally sit down with the problem employee and discuss the matter you've been sitting on for a while, you are released.

The other is to mindfully acknowledge our bad faith. Slow your thinking down a bit and consciously say to yourself or to others something like, "Yes, I've been kidding myself about that." Then explore it. Crack it open and shine the light on it. You may choose to continue your strategy of inaction, but at least you're choosing it. Choosing is good.

GOOD FAITH AND AGENCY

With the future coming at you, you have choices. You have the ability to manage your self-talk and sidestep your fear and defensiveness. You have the choice to shine the light on your bad faith and dissolve it. These are the choices of good faith.

As we said, the dictionary defines "agency" as "action personified," and that's what we're talking about: a person who is not looking to attribute blame but looking to act on their challenges instead.

As a leader, your goal is to encourage your employees to be agents who take responsibility for their results, and action to improve their results. Your success in creating agents among your employees is, not surprisingly, driven by the extent to which you set a good example. By being an agent yourself, you motivate your employees to follow. Self-management is the key: train your brain to respond as an agent and you'll be surrounded by agents.

SELF-ACCEPTANCE, SELF-EXPOSURE

When you're acting in good faith, you put all your most difficult or embarrassing truths out there because you have nothing to hide. You're confident enough to know that your flaws and your mistakes do not invalidate you as a person. Your self-esteem is high enough that your ego doesn't need to protect you by hiding the "shameful" truth about yourself from other people.

You can adopt a kind of transcendent view of the whole package — who you are, what the situation is really all about — all without any ego.

Good faith is that beautiful country beyond the borders of ego. The citizens of that country are not afraid of the facts and always allow the truth to fully inform their stance and approach.

WHAT COMMITMENT LOOKS LIKE

When you are committed in this way, here is how people see you:

1. You live by your word
2. You spend no time allocating blame, because, for you, blame does not exist. Commitment and fulfillment exist. When something goes wrong, you move to fix it. Action is the name of your game
3. As a person who is gaining authority over the meta-level dynamics of your mind (a person who manages your self-talk, opinions, and judgments), you don't get lost in worry. You choose faith. You will succeed. You know it

4. You don't hide in a false projection. You expose yourself with nothing to hide. You are okay as you are

5. You are aware of your brain's proclivity to live in bad faith on matters and you step in to override it.

INSPIRING COMMITMENT IN OTHERS

Surely these things will make you a great role model for commitment. There's a wonderful consequence to giving your team a view of how committed people operate. Not only do they know and aspire toward how people like you operate in the world, they also feel the favorable effects. They don't feel judged or targeted for blame. They know they can count on you to keep your word. They feel heard and valued.

But, aside from role modeling, how do you actually cause others to feel committed to you and the organization?

That takes us back to the Paradox of Influence. You cause commitment to you by making your conversations about them. It makes sense, when you think about it.

Remember, from chapter five, Erich Fromm's point that we are all seeking to feel heard? We were once connected to our mothers, but now we are alone. Sure, we have our family, our friends, but no matter how you cut it, we have our aloneness. It's like waking in the middle of the night while all around us are off in slumber.

In the same way that plants move toward the light, people move toward connection. We can't force connection on them. It must be in their language, so to speak; shy people, for example, don't want you prying away, they want an ever-so-delicate nod to their desire to be left alone. But they want that nod.

We all want that nod. That's one way to get people committed to us and our organization.

There are many ways to offer that recognition. Engaging in conversation. Empathizing in conversation! Supporting self-esteem. Supporting the person in reaching their goals.

Even demonstrating your own humanity contributes to getting people to follow you with a sense of commitment. Thus, full-disclosure communication, where you indicate your feelings of vulnerability in offering complete information, draws people toward you. It must be genuine. People can smell fraudulent statements of vulnerability, as in, "It sure hurts me to tell you this, Billy, it hurts me deep, but gosh, I think you're not working so hard these days."

Authenticity is the best way to demonstrate your humanity. Just being honest, straight with somebody, can lead to a powerful sense of commonality. When people recognize that you have the same dark nights that they do — and we all have our dark nights — a deep, human sense of commonality or trust emerges in the relationship. What a profound way to nod! Let them recognize that you and they have humanity in common.

Of course, this is not to say you don't need to actually ask for commitment. Indeed, getting people to live by their word includes asking for their word. But only after you've connected with and to some extent addressed the employee's cravings and fears.

Asking for a commitment to things helps people to stay away from their own bad faith. It's as simple as: "So it sounds like we have a plan. Are you okay with all of this? When do you think you'll have phase one completed?"

ACCOUNTABILITY

When you've got a team of committed people, you have created a culture of accountability. This means people hold themselves to account for how they perform against their commitments. A culture of accountability is a culture in which leaders, managers, and employees together focus on results, which is the focus of the next part of this book.

In such a culture, people are open to being observed because they aren't fearful of blame or the personal judgments of an ego-based leader. They are more likely to be agents, seeking to act on challenges rather than defensively attributing blame or fearfully reciting all the things that may go wrong. They are people of high self-esteem, because their leader supports them. As a result, they are exemplars of will, declaring their intentions and fulfilling them. Just like that.

It is to this level of mastery, and its practical effects, that we now turn.

PART III

MASTERY

■

CHAPTER NINE

HAVING GREAT CONVERSATIONS

In this concluding part of the book you're going to see how everything we've discussed — how you can manage yourself and lead your people from a selfless place — can come alive for you and your team, with remarkable results. We are assuming that the concepts and practices are becoming part of your natural way of operating on the job.

I think of the example of a young NHL hockey team that is on an arc to becoming a winning team. At first they have to be conscious of every move they make and every strategy they take. They are, in a sense, one step behind the action as, in the hurly burly of a game, they constantly bring their coaches' dicta to mind and try to avoid mistakes.. However, sports color commentators will say of them later, when they are racking up win after win, "Look at them play. They're *mindless* out there!"

To a large extent that's what we're talking about in the last chapters of this book: leaders who no longer have to look at the angle of their sticks and remember not to ice the puck when they have a man advantage, leaders who manage themselves and others in such a way that a commentator could say, "Look at those leaders; they're *egoless* out there!

Specifically, in this chapter we'll look at how leaders beyond ego are primarily not coaches or managers or consultants, important as all those roles are, but *facilitators*. This shows up primarily in the conversations they have with those who work with them. We'll explore how leaders can converse so they are facilitating employees to move along the path toward goals.

In the following chapter, we'll examine the kind of culture that can be created departmentally and organizationally when leaders at the top of their game expertly resolve tensions and challenges from a mountaintop perspective beyond ego.

Then, in the final chapter of the book, we will drill down to answer the question of whether all of this theory actually works in the real world of business today.

THE FINESSE OF FACILITATION

When you are at your best, with ego set aside and in flow with your role, you interact with others — both in groups and one-on-one — with a certain kind of adroitness. Some examples:

- You ask more and tell less
- You refer to what you have just heard from someone as you communicate your ideas to them ("To your point, Stefano . . .")
- You are less likely to attribute blame and more likely to take full responsibility for problems
- You are less likely to dominate and more likely to pull others into discussion

The biggest sign of leadership finesse is that you don't push people, you pull them. You deal with people on your team in a wide array of situations, but pulling, not pushing, is the overarching theme.

Speaking of the diverse nature of your role, let's get some terms clear so we're in the same place. For our purposes:

- *Managing* is about control. When you are the manager, you are in charge. As manager, you make sure things are under control
- *Leading* is about providing a vision, inspiring people, keeping them on track
- *Consulting* is about giving advice. When someone on your team consults you, they are seeking your sage advice
- *Coaching* is about causing growth in others. When you coach your team members, you are trying to develop them. They grow when you introduce them to new things and to patterns you have observed in their own behavior
- *Facilitating* is about making things happen easily and about drawing things out of others

These are all functions of being a boss. At times you manage; at other times you lead. Hopefully, you coach. Surely you play the role of consultant, giving advice as required. Sometimes you facilitate things for people, in both senses of the word: you do things behind the scenes to "grease the wheels," and you use questions to open people up and move discussion forward. This latter kind of facilitating itself falls into two sub-categories: one-on-one and in groups.

Facilitating one-on-one is what you are called on to do as a leader every day. We'll talk a lot more about this later.

As for facilitating a group, let's consider it for a moment. It's pretty interesting. Some leaders do it a lot and others don't. It depends on the type of role you fill. If you are the manager of a variety store, for example, you may not find yourself in a board-room getting your employees to brainstorm solutions to a common problem. Your job is to make sure the store is running smoothly, people are doing their jobs, and things are under control. However, even when the variety store manager gets herself beyond ego, she exercises this facilitator skill set. It equates to "more pull, less push."

My firm employs facilitators and I've seen and worked with several I would call "masters." They've been doing it for years and have excellent reputations for getting superlative results. Let's take a moment to look at what they do. Then we'll consider the skills they need in order to facilitate well and see how these apply to leadership in general.

The term "facilitator" as it applies to a person leading discussion at the front of the room has two main senses: it could be an educator or trainer who is trying to cause learning for each individual in the room, or it could be someone who is trying to get the room of people to reach some group agreements. My firm actually provides both services to clients. Sometimes we are educators; sometimes we're leading discussions.

When we are educating, we may be helping salespeople develop their selling skills or leaders to enhance their coaching skills. When we are leading discussions, we may be getting a group to self-reflect on how they would like to change certain processes or how they could improve as a group of peers. We are basically trying to harness the brainpower in the room to bear down on a certain question or problem.

I dare say that facilitating discussion is more challenging than providing instruction. Compared with leading people in answering predetermined questions — Where are we strong? Where are we weak? How can we leverage our strengths to compensate for our weaknesses? — discussion calls for pretty sophisticated "stand-up" skills.

We will soon see that these are the same skills that you need in order to find finesse as an egoless leader. In fact, we've already considered some of these skills in each chapter of the book.

The facilitator and self-management

In broad terms, effectively facilitating group discussion calls for self-management skills. For example, let's say you're in front of the room and your ego is active. What happens? Self-talk is triggered in the audience as they focus more on you than on the discussion. Indeed, a good facilitator — and an egoless leader — can somehow drive discussion and be invisible at the same time.

This is no small feat. My experience is that when they are doing their work, master facilitators are free of self-consciousness. Their attention is totally external to themselves. They don't see themselves as up against others or even up against a problem. They operate in the moment calling for, sorting out, and taking full advantage of the contributions of others. Their sessions would be much less productive if their egos intruded. Ego is poison to facilitative momentum. For one thing, facilitators don't have the mental bandwidth to deal with the complexity of group sessions when they are trying to deal with their own egos too. Influential leaders self-manage their ego out of the dynamic of the room.

By effectively self-managing in this way, facilitators increase their ability to listen. Great facilitators hear the individuals in their room and make them feel heard.

Another particularly important skill is the ability to use what was just said by somebody as a springboard to move the conversation forward. It's impressive to see this skill in action. You need to know the goal and to recognize an opportunity to reach it based on the thoughts of others. That, of course, links to our chapter on goal alignment.

Yes, even the ability of a facilitator to remain free of personal judgments of participants is critical. (See chapter three.) And every single person in the room must feel supported by the person at the front of the room. (See chapter six.) You have to get beyond ego to accomplish this.

Of course, another skill of facilitation is to make sure people in the group make commitments that they are likely to keep.

Question asking

But the biggest skill of all that master facilitators possess, the skill being focused on in this chapter, is the ability to ask questions. It sounds easy, doesn't it? In fact, the basic questions facilitators walk into the room with *are* somewhat straightforward. Facilitators know the main questions of a group-think process before they even get to the building where they are going to do their work. That shortlist of questions is called the "architecture" of the session.

You may have heard that the ancient Greek philosopher Socrates was pretty skilful in asking questions. In fact, in one of his dialogues he managed to get an uneducated young boy to understand the Pythagorean theorem — just by asking him questions. He used simple questions like, "If we draw a line diagonally through this square that we've drawn into the sand, young fella, what two shapes have we created?" The young boy would answer something like, "We would have two triangles, oh wise one." Socrates would come back with a question about the line that both triangles share, and explore — through questions — how that line was longer than the other two sides of each of the triangles. And on he would go, taking the boy through the logic of the theorem. Over 2000 years later we still see the "Socratic method" as a pretty special way of moving people.

For master facilitators, question asking involves:

- Picking up on cues from participants that there is a nugget underneath what they are saying
- Knowing when to drill deeper into someone's answers
- Knowing how to phrase a question so it is most provocative or useful
- Recognizing the paradigm of someone answering a question and knowing the exact little thing they need to hear to expand (or even explode) that paradigm
- Mastering timing: knowing when there is a readiness to wrestle with

the next big question, and determining with the group what specifically needs to be explored during a predetermined period of time

So here's the idea behind the finesse of facilitation: When you are beyond ego, you interact with people — whether one-on-one or in groups — like a master facilitator. You move people through the quality of your questioning. You educate them. You provoke them. You get them to do their own thinking. You get them to commit. And all this by what you ask rather than by what you say. I haven't met anyone with the bandwidth to accomplish all this when in an ego state.

As you would guess, one is engaging an underlying methodology when using questions to educate people or move them toward some goal. You can't just ask random questions and you can't always ask even the best questions out of order. But what is this methodology?

BEING RATIONAL

In a business context, all our discussions tend to follow a rational agenda. Sometimes the agenda items are unspoken or taken for granted and sometimes they are overt. The agenda basically addresses goals and plans to reach them. Very simple. You do this pretty much every day. For example, if I was seated next to you while you are reading this book, I might ask you, "What's your goal in reading this book?" And then, in response to what you tell me, I might ask what challenges you face in reaching that goal. Next I would want to know what you could do to improve your ability to overcome those challenges. Ultimately, to bring you value, I would ask if you were willing to undertake those steps. If so, we'd move to commitment.

This is a garden-variety rational business dialogue. In business, something is rational if it efficiently helps to reach a goal. If I want a coffee and there is a viable source just down the hall, but

I go outside for one (and I don't particularly want to go outside or spend more time getting my caffeine hit), then my behavior is not rational because it's not efficient.

The line of thinking we're talking about is termed by some philosophers "goal-directed rationality" (GDR). It is not a particularly profound or complex notion, but that doesn't mean it's an easy thinking process to grab onto. Left to their own devices, an individual or a team is easily subverted by fears, self-talk, confusion, and so on. This is why facilitation is so important. Done right, it's a graceful, efficient means of guiding all the best efforts of our employees toward rational outcomes.

The basic sequence for facilitating via GDR is:

- Define the *goal*
- Define the *obstacles* or challenges
- Define the *resources* or means to remove the obstacles or overcome the challenges
- Make a *plan* that leverages those possibilities
- *Commit* to the plan and ultimately *act* on it
- Then *re-evaluate* and do it all again on an ongoing basis

As a leader you facilitate your people's progress within the framework of GDR. We could call it the foundational paradigm of your functional business relationships.

For example, if you were promoted to a new management position and you were meeting your people one-on-one, your first logical question would be, "What are you working on these days?" Get the goal out, and the obstacles, and you're rolling. Or, if you are trying to solve a problem with an employee, you revisit the goal, figure out the cause of the problem, look at ways to put the problem to rest, and make a plan. Or, if you are coaching someone, you might uncover their short-term or long-term goal and proceed to help them achieve it as they go about fulfilling the organization's goals. The versatility of the model is unquestionable.

There are many versions of GDR. For example, you've probably heard of the "gap analysis," where you define the ideal state concerning some matter and compare that with where you are now and make a plan to close the gap. Salespeople basically use GDR to manage their way through a sales call. Presenters sometimes use some version of GDR to organize their thoughts and delivery agenda. And then there are those who prefer to address problems rather than goals. But it's all really the same thing. Instead of starting with the goal, they're starting with a statement of the problem to be solved. This is considered just another version of GDR because, of course, when you have a problem, the goal is to solve it. And, when you have a goal, the problem is that you're not there yet.

But we're not at our main point yet. You probably use GDR in some form all the time. It's how rational people operate. The trick is to do it on purpose and to allow GDR to inform your questioning. It becomes your questioning direction tool. The questions themselves have to be posed in the most productive way. And gracefully.

"Gracefully" won't be possible if you see yourself as above, against, or below the people who work for you. If you see yourself as exerting force on them from the outside, then your people rightly interpret your leadership as laying down goals and insisting that they embrace them. They see you as enunciating a goal and then pointing out obstacles (through judgments), dulling any allure that the goal may have had for them and extinguishing any inspiration they may have felt to get there together. They see you as forcing them to use certain resources. If this is your style, you are basically dehumanizing your employees, holding them hostage for exhibiting behaviors, taking actions, producing results.

Being graceful about it means nudging and nurturing. It

means finding out what's important to your employees and putting their passions into play to work for you. It means using a thoughtful, intuition-based tactical approach.

This is not to say there's no room for management or control, or measurement or accountability. But when you lead beyond ego, you do these things gracefully. The idea is that you want to nurture people along a GDR track through dialogue rather than telling them how things ought to be.

A QUESTION-ASKING CONVERSATION

Let's look at facilitation in action. (After the conversation we'll go over it step by step and see how things went.)

Susan is a sales leader at a wine distributor, New World Wines. She reports to John, the Chief Operating Officer. Susan's counterpart in the marketing department is named Fernando.

> JOHN: I would like to talk about how things are going between your team and the marketing group.
>
> SUSAN: Sure.
>
> JOHN: I'm wondering about the alignment of the two departments.
>
> SUSAN: How so?
>
> JOHN: Well, I saw this one customer communication going out from one of your reps and it doesn't really align with marketing's strategy. And I've seen this sort of thing before.
>
> SUSAN: What do you mean?
>
> JOHN: Well, since the big push this spring season is the mid-range boxed wines, marketing is asking that all e-mail communications to customers go out on a light green background with the picnic watermark and the keywords "light" and "fresh."
>
> SUSAN: Right . . .
>
> JOHN: The thing is, I came across a forwarded message from Sam's computer last week that was still using the blue background and the penguin design from last winter's Chilean sparkling wine push.

SUSAN: Oh.

JOHN: The truth is that I don't know whether this is a recurring theme or not. And this particular instance is not particularly important to me. But it did remind me of the old notion that the tactics of marketing intersect with the strategy of sales. There is a forced interface there and it involves mutual cooperation. I'm wondering how that's going.

SUSAN: Well . . . they distribute the monthly marketing communiqués. And Fernando and I sometimes catch up at the Friday-morning meeting. I'm honestly not sure what more we could do. Sam's a good guy, you know that. I'm sure it was an honest mistake.

JOHN: I get that, but I'm wondering about the bigger picture. By definition some amount of time must be spent standing at the fence between the two realms of sales and marketing. Tell me about that interface. Is it a happy fence line? Talk to me about this.

SUSAN: You know what my guys are like. When they find something that works for them, they like to stick with it. Sometimes the marketing promotions don't hit the mark. So there is a bit of a balancing act. We take guidance and we generally roll out as planned, but there's nothing like actually being on the street to know what customers really want. Marketing sometimes just isn't connected enough.

JOHN: And what would marketing folks say about sales?

SUSAN: We had that discussion at last year's conference, if you recall. Their view was that we weren't rigorous enough.

JOHN: And where's the truth?

SUSAN: Obviously somewhere in the middle. But I think there's been some movement.

JOHN: How so?

SUSAN: Since last year, there's been more product training. Product managers come out on more sales calls. I think there's improved communication overall.

JOHN: Good. I'm glad to hear that. Have you noticed the effects of those things?

SUSAN: Well, there might be a little less stress. It's hard to tell. We have a lot on the go. Have you heard that there are issues?

JOHN: What I'm sure of is that how well you guys connect is pretty key. I think we'd be smart to pay attention to it.

SUSAN: Well, I can talk to my guys about it.

JOHN: Good. But I want your insight. What do *you* think?

SUSAN: I think we have so much going on most of the time that I lose sight of the issue. That's the truth of it. As we said a couple of weeks ago, I don't step back to see the bigger picture enough. This is another example of that.

JOHN: I see. And that conversation, if I recall, linked to the topic of stress as well. Perhaps you're right about the need to step back. What do you want to do about it, when it comes to marketing?

SUSAN: Maybe I should have a meeting with Fernando to talk about greater alignment. We can see how it goes.

JOHN: Good. And maybe the three of us can get together after that to look at what you came up with.

SUSAN: Sure. It's a plan. I'll arrange for us to meet within the next couple of weeks.

JOHN: Good. Are you okay with this conversation?

SUSAN: Sure. I appreciate it, actually. I don't step back enough.

JOHN: Why don't we meet again separately to talk about how you're doing with that in particular? I'd like to support you on it.

SUSAN: Okay. I'll book it.

THE PLAY-BY-PLAY

Now, taking into account everything we've covered so far in this book, here's a tactical play-by-play of the conversation John and Susan just had.

GDR (Goal-Directed Rationality): What are they trying to facilitate?

The backdrop to the conversation is this: John is a leader who knows that one of his sales leaders, Susan, doesn't seem to get along with Fernando, leader of the marketing group. John needs the two of them to work in harmony, yet they seem to operate in silos.

John's goal coming into the conversation? He needs to get to why this is the case, and he needs to get Susan started on the path to figuring out this problem. Basically, the two of them need to define the obstacles to harmony and to implement a plan for improving the situation.

Susan's goal or unspoken craving coming into the conversation? To manage stress more effectively.

Notice how the multiple goals are all being addressed in this conversation. John is dealing with his boss's angst over alignment as well as with his own desire to optimize alignment. And he is weaving Susan's cravings — reduced stress in her life — into the discussion. Both win. That's goal-alignment.

But what about the process of goal-directed rationality? Let's look at the leader's (facilitator's) questions in the context of the flow of GDR.

> **Goals:** John put the goal for the discussion onto the table quickly by saying he wanted to talk about the alignment of sales and marketing. Alignment is the goal.

> **Obstacles:** John gave an example of an obstacle to that goal fulfillment: non-compliance on the part of at least one sales rep on one occasion. John and Susan also considered the alleged lack of rigor on the part of the sales team as a possible obstacle.

> **Resources:** John and Susan looked briefly at things that have been done so far (sales training and sales calls, possible improved communication).

> **Plan:** Because they don't have enough information about the obstacles and resources, they made a plan to collect the thoughts of Susan

and Fernando and subsequently to put their three heads together on the matter.

Commit and Act: Susan will arrange for the meetings.

Re-evaluate: They will re-evaluate at future meetings.

Of course, there is another whole layer of goal-directed thinking woven into the dialogue. Put succinctly, the cited obstacle in front of Susan's goal of getting control of the stress in her life was defined partly as not stepping back enough to see the big picture. John is one resource she can call on to deal with that obstacle and the two have made a plan and commitments to execute the plan.

So, let's review for a moment. A leader met with a team member and used GDR to guide his way though a conversation. In the process goals were aligned (his goal of alignment and her craving for improved stress management). But other things described in previous chapters came to life as well. Let's consider them.

Full disclosure

John is not disclosing the fact that his boss (the CEO of New World Wines) saw Sam's email and came into John's office fuming. It's better if John doesn't involve Susan in those politics.

However, John is sharing with Susan the key facts of the situation: a non-compliant email went out; it's not, in itself, a big deal; it could be the tip of the iceberg (John's boss definitely thought it was); we need to be focused on optimizing alignment.

Being non-judgmental

For any of this stuff to work — for Susan to listen, reflect, and learn — John knows he has to be non-judgmental. This minimizes the chances of Susan's being defensive.

There are two rules here:

- No generalizations
- Don't dwell on particular instances

John begins the conversation, therefore, with a comment that's neutral and conceptual: "I would like to talk about how things are going between your team and the marketing group."

Next, trying to minimize any generalization he may be making, he says: "I'm wondering about the alignment of the two departments." Notice he's not certain about this idea. How can he be? He's only testing a hypothesis. He knows about the Subjective Truth Syndrome: that he might see only what his own beliefs dictate.

Sticking to purely factual judgments, John says: "Well, I saw this one customer communication going out from one of your reps and it doesn't really align with marketing's strategy. And I've seen this sort of thing before."

With this Susan may get a little fidgety. Her self-talk may start to run. She may get a little defensive. But John hasn't actually judged her; he's just putting out the facts.

However, anticipating what may be going through Susan's head, John tries to back off a little. He says, "The truth is that I don't know whether this is a recurring theme or not. And this particular instance is not particularly important to me. But it did remind me of the old notion that the tactics of marketing intersect with the strategy of sales. There is a forced interface there and it involves mutual cooperation." By saying this John makes sure he's not dwelling on a particular instance. He keeps the focus on what they can do going forward.

From this point on in the conversation things should open up. John has taken some risks in guiding the conversation in this way, but he has been careful to stay completely factual and avoid blaming.

Demonstrating empathy

Empathy, as we've seen, is the art of seeing the world as the other person sees it. So, after John detects some diffidence from Susan when he talks about Sam's gaffe, he empathizes a little. His sense is that the tactical side of marketing touches the strategic part of selling, so some degree of head butting between the two departments is natural. He's guessing that this dynamic is affecting Susan's ability to work effectively with Fernando and his department.

He tests out this theory by saying: "By definition some amount of time must be spent standing at the fence between the two realms."

If he says this, and he's right, then he has made Susan feel understood. This is also an opportunity for him to coax Susan in the direction of growth, so he continues with: "Tell me about that interface. Is it a happy fence line?"

Probing for feelings

Although John wasn't expecting any resentment from Susan, he did ask her at the end if she was okay with the conversation. This gives her a chance to express herself. Sometimes such an inquiry yields valuable information and the opportunity for the leader to make the employee feel heard.

In this case, it reminded John that she could probably use more support on the stress-management mission of hers. So they agreed to a discussion.

Asking good questions

Do you have to know more than the person whose growth you are facilitating? No, you just have to ask good questions. John doesn't know anything special about Susan and Fernando's situation. All he has is a hunch, a goal, and a few tactical tools at his disposal.

Most of us know the difference between open questions and closed questions. Open questions beg for the other person to get talking (why, how). Closed questions (do, can, will, are, did, have, has, is) can be answered with one word. Asking open questions is a useful basic skill.

Piggyback questions are also handy. You say something that sets the context of the question, that tells the person where to take their answer. "By definition some amount of time must be spent standing at the fence between the two realms. Tell me about that interface. Is it a happy fence line?"

The tougher skill is to ask insightful, open questions. To do this, you benefit from having a hypothesis and from using open questions, often piggybacked, to test it. In the conversation above, John came in with an impression that perhaps sales and marketing weren't talking and that part of the blockage was coming from the perspectives of the respective leaders. Then he started asking Susan questions to figure out whether his hunch was right.

Facilitating

Notice how John is facilitating growth. He's doing several things at once, but all at the behest of what he wants to facilitate:

- He's *leading*, because he has a vision of the harmony he is seeking
- He's *coaching*, getting Susan to reflect on themes or a pattern and thereby causing her to grow. The insight his questioning might draw out could be, "Hmmm, that's true, I am sort of territorial." He's also helping her to gain a deeper understanding of how sales and marketing can interface
- He's *managing*. According to his boss, he has a problem and he is moving to get control of things. In the nicest possible way. The end result of the dialogue is Susan's commitment to schedule a joint meeting about this in the next couple of weeks

And John is doing these things not with himself at the center of things; the issue is at the center of things. John addresses the issue while attending to the other person's needs. This is leading beyond ego.

THE ESSENCE OF FACILITATIVE QUESTIONING

What makes a question insightful? We said above that it can involve having a hypothesis and testing it with a question. For example, if I think you are getting tired of this chapter, I might ask, "How are you doing with this chapter?" That question steers us in the direction of gathering information with regard to my hypothesis. But let's take this apart a bit more.

An insightful question is one that concerns some phase or step in the GDR thinking process. Sometimes you have a hypothesis or tentative belief around the answer and sometimes you don't. But your question is insightful if it is:

- Moving in deeper to define a challenge (or goal or problem)
- Determining roadblocks (or obstacles, barriers, causes)
- Uncovering possible routes to take (which resources are available)
- Making a plan

For example, here are some presumably insightful questions concerning your goal in reading this book:

- Why are you reading this book?
- What is it about you that makes the topic interesting to you?
- What is your growth opportunity when it comes to your leadership style?
- Why do you want to grow in this area?
- Do you *really* want to grow in this area?

These questions are meant to uncover your goal when it comes to your leadership development.

With that goal clearly defined, and embraced, I can now ask

you questions about what's holding you back from achieving this goal. If I ask about this by using open questions, I will get to your circumstances. Answering honestly, you will probably describe the challenges you face. Perhaps we'll trace it back to your having been told you've got a big ego, and further back to your belief that you didn't get enough reinforcement as a kid. Who knows? What we do know is that the GDR agenda will eventually get you to useful answers or elevated self-knowledge.

The interesting thing is that the degree of your honesty will dictate the amount of value you get from our dialogue. That's why it's important for the facilitator to listen carefully for authenticity.

We said that as leader, you create value by walking someone through a GDR thinking process. By value, I mean advantage or the possibility of advantage. That's the effect that you cause as a facilitator. The recipients of your effort are advantaged through the quality of your insightful questions. So too is the employer.

Questions pull people. Demands push. Asking is probably harder work, which means there's an impulse not to do it. Once again, self-management is central to your day-to-day role as influential leader.

■

CHAPTER TEN

SEEING THINGS FROM
THE MOUNTAINTOP

Visualize this.

You lead a team of people who feel heard by you. So they have a sense of personal connection and satisfaction. They feel touched that you know what they're trying to achieve for themselves. Perhaps you know their fears and the things they crave. They know your goals for them and they are in touch with the mission. They feel valued by you. They recognize your commitment and that you mean your word. You expect them to mean their word too.

A LEADER'S PERSPECTIVE

Imagine yourself as a leader in this culture. A key element of your leadership is the perspective you have of yourself. You see yourself not as the star of the show but as the one who brings together seemingly disparate views. This perspective has come about as you have redirected your attention:

- From your self-talk to the other person (empathy)
- From your strong opinions and judgments to the facts of the matter
- From your need to get what you want to the needs of others to feel big rather than small (supporting self-esteem)
- From your own goal to the creative challenge of finding the

overarching answer to both parties' goals (goal alignment)
- From why things can't work to how they can work
- From what the past is responsible for to what the future calls for (avoiding a blame culture and imbuing a sense of agency)

Now you can go a step further, developing a mind that's like a solution-seeking missile. A mind that heads unerringly past the "or" of business as usual to the "and" that makes business truly unusual.

Developing this perspective is not easy. Ego always manages to find a way to creep into the proceedings. Ego — representing the vantage point of being below, above, or against others or circumstances — sees things as black or white, not both. Ego is stubborn. Its instinct is to subtract or divide, not to add or multiply. To ego, a unifying perspective is just plain counter-intuitive.

But as you continue to move beyond ego, you will be up to the challenge of developing this perspective, solving problems and transforming them into opportunities and results.

A couple of chapters ago I quoted my friend as saying, "It's all in the 'and.'" We've already seen how this principle comes into play when you set your ego aside as you deal with your team members. You hear where they are coming from, you know what you need, and you find a higher-level position that satisfies both needs.

This bigger, more inclusive perspective is more likely to see the resolution of paradoxes.

Zen masters actually use paradoxes (called "koans") to snap their monks out of their narrow perspectives. They try to jar their students into a more all-encompassing orientation. We're not going to approach this perspective from the level of startling you in order to crack you open. We're going to look at some accessible descriptions of how you can adopt it.

A paradox is a statement that seems self-contradictory but in reality expresses a possible truth.

The escape from all good paradoxes is to find a way to make both seemingly contradictory elements true. Usually we are stuck in a perspective where paradoxes don't make sense. Getting unstuck, seeing the overarching principle behind the paradox, requires us to step out of our egocentric perspective.

From the Mountaintop of Perspective . . .

A lot of references in this book have been made to this different perspective. We've said that you must get "beyond ego," you must "transcend" ego, and you must "rise above" a problem and get to a "higher" place in order to see the "overarching" idea or point of view. It's time we brought greater clarity to these references.

Are you familiar with the word "dialectic"? It's a fancy term for how ideas evolve. For example, somebody makes the claim, "The key to producing results is to focus on goals." Some people hearing that claim may think it's wrong, arguing, "Yes, but when you focus on goals, you ignore the people."

What do we have here? Two opposing arguments. As a result of the tension between them, both parties may hash it out and agree on something like: "The key to producing results is to focus on goals while tending to the needs of the people who are tackling them."

That final idea is sometimes referred to as the synthesis of the two arguments that led to it. So you've got argument one, leading to the counterargument (argument two), leading to an overarching conclusion that honors both sides.

And it doesn't stop there. That new idea, the synthesis, becomes a new arguable position that inevitably yields it counterargument. A new polarity arises. It is transcended. Evolution continues.

Using our example above, when somebody hears, "The key to producing results is to focus on goals while tending to the needs of the people who are tackling them," they may counter with,

"Yes, but we don't just want any results, we want optimal results, results that define success!" They hash it out, and a new idea is born.

Here's the good news about all this. Changing your approach as a result of dialectic doesn't necessarily require you to negate anything you've done before.

Take coaching, for example. I often teach coaching skills to groups of leaders who are highly task oriented. They come into the session thinking that they are already fine coaches. They hear in advance that they are going to learn about empathy and they are skeptical.

But in the session, they learn that they weren't really coaching at all. Their coaching sessions were actually opportunities to manage, to keep things under control. Here's what they thought was coaching:

An employee enters their office for a regular coaching session.
BOSS: Okay, last time we met we talked about you making more cold calls. You agreed to make twenty extra calls this week. How did that go?
EMPLOYEE: Gulp!

This is not coaching; it's control.

What these leaders learn is that they need to infuse a relationship-orientation or other-orientation into their dialogues. Conversations can be about the same topic as before, but now need to be about how the employee feels about that topic. From that context, the two can move toward goals.

The notion of the dialectic bringing a solution to a problem by reconciling the tension between opposites is a good illustration of the solution-generating perspective that you as an influential leader can adopt. It's as if there is a place in your mind where you can see ideas coming together. It's not an ego place because instead of dividing, it *conjoins*. It's a place where you bring things together. The perfect place from which to see solutions to problems.

... To the Valley of Problems

I like to classify problems into three types: It Problems, Is/Ought Problems, and And Problems. Let's look at each type.

It Problems

These problems have two characteristics: they become worse and worse; and they have no upsides. Having an incurable disease is an It problem. So is running out of cash. From the point of view of ego management, there's not much we are going to say about this type of problem other than this: The future is coming at you. Rather than becoming idle as you emotionally process what will be, you need to move into action. Don't see yourself as up against it; see yourself instead as the agent who is making things happen.

But be careful to check your assumptions. What you may see as an It problem could be something else. That criterion of its not having an upside is pretty important. For example, if your marriage is failing, it's an It problem. But if your marriage is failing and you discover an upside to that, then it's still a problem, but it's an Is/Ought problem.

Is/Ought Problems

Is/Ought problems are usually grounded in complaints. What *is*, is not okay; things *ought* to be different. There is the current circumstance, and there is the way we think things ought to be. Traffic in Manhattan is a good example of this type of problem. The *is* pertains to how busy it is. The *ought* pertains to the traffic rules or congestion tax that I think they should establish. In Is/Ought problems, there is always an upside to the *is* component. For example, we have to admit that the upside of Manhattan traffic is that it facilitates an economic machine that helps many millions of people pursue a better life.

- People say my handwriting is a problem. And it is. Sometimes it's illegible. That's the *is* side of the polarity. But for me, the upside to the mess is that it allows me to write quickly. The *ought* side of the polarity is obviously that I should write more neatly
- Raoul is stubborn. He ought to be flexible. The upside of his stubbornness is that he stands his ground on important matters
- Beulah is crabby at times. She is sometimes hard to be around. She ought to be friendly. There is an upside to her crabbiness, though. Beulah is only crabby when something means a lot to her. Her crabbiness actually reflects a level of dedication
- Lawrence hates to be controlled by others. So he is tough to manage. He ought to be more compliant. The upside, however, is that his independent spirit makes him great behind the scenes, making things happen. And he's easy to delegate to
- A close relative, Paulie, comes to you asking for advice. He's a wreck. He just got started in the retail business and bought a whole load of product that nobody wants to buy. He's so stressed, he's almost catatonic. The upside is that he's learning about the importance of minimizing risk

Here's the beauty of Is/Ought problems. When you redirect your attention from your anchored ego position of the judgment or the crisis to the upside of the is and the desirability of the ought, you are in a position be non-judgmental and generate solutions.

Let's revisit the examples, keeping in mind that the idea is for you to generate a strategy that seeks out and retains the upside of the *is* and fulfills the beauty of the *ought*.

- Regarding my handwriting, talk to me about how pleased you are that my speedy handwriting keeps me on top of what transpires in meetings. You want to hold onto that advantage *and* you know I agree that legibility is important. Move me toward a solution

- Regarding Raoul's darn stubbornness, help him see that it is laudable when it comes to things that are important. Get him to recognize that even he would agree that he's inflexible on some matters that aren't that important. Get him to understand that his opportunity for growth lies in recognizing the difference

- Regarding Beulah's crabbiness, express your gratitude for her dedication. Celebrate it with her. As you did with Raoul, help her to differentiate when it's prudent and when it does her a disservice

- The same goes for Lawrence. Demonstrate respect for his behind-the-scenes facilitation of progress. Get him to see that his independent streak fuels that advantage. Like all characteristics, it has good and not-so-good aspects. His opportunity is to explore with you when it does you and the team a disservice and when it brings great value

- As for Paulie, who can't see the forest for the trees right now, highlight the upside of the education he's getting. Things are unfolding as they tend to for new retailers. Over time, they learn the tricks. Get him to find out what others do when they have inventory they cannot move. Help him rise above the angst by seeing the upside

All of these approaches rely on the conjoining orientation. You are essentially positioning the Is/Ought problem as a human condition with upsides and downsides. You are demonstrating patience with the employee's human struggle because you have loads of similar struggles. You no longer see the problem as a sin that someone intends and that must be expunged. You see it as just one more example that life is filled with polarities that resolve themselves as the dialectic rolls on. You are the facilitator of the resolution.

And Problems

Some problems exist when two (or more) things that don't present difficulties in and of themselves are combined.

- My son said, "I want to do well in school and I like to play. My teacher said I can't have both." I responded, "Both things are true. How can you have both?"

- I heard a business leader recently lament the constant battle between sales and credit: Sales folks need to get as many customers in the door as possible. And credit folks need to block as much bad credit as they can. Both things are true, and when they come together, it's a source of ongoing stress for all

Hold Both

As with Is/Ought problems, adopting a conjoining orientation is the best way to visualize solutions to And problems. Here is an excellent route to developing a conjoining orientation. It comes from a psychotherapeutic exercise that I have heard referred to as "hold both."

I remember being in a therapist's office sweating over the tension I felt deep inside that my family needs were in significant opposition to my work needs. I felt such stress! My therapist made me stand up and hold out my palms. She said I should imagine placing all my work responsibilities in one palm and all my home responsibilities in the other.

"Okay, feel the weight of the work hand," she said.

I could feel it. It was weighing me down.

"Now, feel the weight of the family hand," she told me.

My heavy work hand started bouncing as I felt the weightiness of my home life.

"Now, hold both."

I allowed my attention to experience both heavy hands. I

stood there for a few moments. I brought my hands together as though needing two hands to hold one object. It began to sink in that I was holding both. My brain somehow started to synthesize both. I was integrating. I was seeing the "and" rather than the "either/or." I began to visualize work/life balance solutions from a place in my head that was already there. It was a great experience. I was redirecting my attention from the angst of a polarity to the peacefulness of unifying two seeming opposites.

The Personal Value Paradox

Here's another example of an And problem and how the conjoining orientation can be applied to resolve it. It concerns the tension many of us feel between how society evaluates us based on how we perform, while in our hearts we know that our value is not in our performance. Let's see how we can redirect our attention away from the tension inherent in that polarity and put it on holding both.

We do value people based on how they perform. I don't just mean that we pay them more, although we do. We value them in our hearts. I know a family doctor who burns himself out dedicating his life to the well-being of his patients. I've heard many people exclaim, "Oh, he's such a good man!" I know a corporate leader, way up at the peak of a huge mountain of a company. The esteem with which people view him, because of his power and what he has accomplished, is profound. He is valued by society — the media, the charitable boards on which he sits, the public at large — in a manner that says, "Now *there's* a valued member of society."

Many people value themselves based on their performance. I have colleagues who are hard on themselves when they do not perform. They beat themselves up. I have friends who see themselves pretty highly as a result of the professional heights they have climbed. I know a young man who compares himself with his father. He feels deflated because, no matter what his father says, he still firmly believes that he will never measure up to him.

My point is not that ego is a problem for these people — it may or may not be. My point is that there is a paradigm most of us operate within that values people based on their performance.

The performance paradigm starts when we're kids. Little Jimmy is good because he shares. You should share too. Jimmy got six out of eight on his spelling test. Let's see if we can get Jimmy's score to go up. He's going to have to do better in school if he wants to get into that special program. He's going to have to do well at the basketball tryouts if he's going to make the team. He's going to have to rise to the top of his class if he wants to get the best job. Look how well Jimmy's brother is doing. Jimmy is going to have to be darned sharp on the job to get that next promotion, the next increase in pay level. And on and on it goes.

It's built right into Charles Darwin's survival-of-the-fittest principle. We say that in the jungle, only the strong survive. That makes sense. The smart ones do rise to the top.

The other truth in the paradox is that at some level we all know better. A parent with two children, one a genius and one average, doesn't have less love for the average child (unless, of course, the paradox is unresolved for that parent). The parent loves and values both offspring equally.

Both sides of the polarity are valid. It's an And problem. We are saying that performance matters. And we are saying that we are allowed to hold unconditional positive regard toward the people on our team. It looks like a paradox.

Well, both points of view can be valid at the same time. Just because I get that you have a lazy streak as long as a meandering country road, and that I can see you as lovable, doesn't mean you get to stay on my team. Or just because you don't like cold-calling prospective customers and you don't do it frequently enough because it just burns your spirit, doesn't mean I'm not counting your calls or calculating the rate at which you convert a prospective customer into a real customer. It means that I am compassionately, maybe patiently, working with you to reach our goals. I'm not sure how patient I can be. But I'm certainly not battering down your door and pushing you to produce. Instead, I am speaking your language. I am staying focused on the facts.

They are both true: I love you *and* you have to produce.

The moral of the story concerning And problems is that our egos often resist reconciling the two parts of such problems. They look like they are in opposition to each other, so we just block ourselves from escape. We fall into a kind of bad faith (see chapter seven), where we lie to ourselves about the inconsistency.

But, in the context of full-disclosure — to the employee and to ourselves — we have nothing to hide. They're both true! Now, let's figure out what we're going to do about it.

The Responsibility Paradox

Still another example of an And problem, and the application of a conjoining orientation, is whether you can visualize a way out of the Responsibility Paradox. For example:

Participants in a project add up to 100% of the labor and each participant owns 100% responsibility for its success.

Or, said another way:

On the one hand we divvy up responsibilities, yet on the other hand we expect that everyone is wholly responsible.

But let's hold both: You are wholly responsible for the success of your piece of your organization *and* you are wholly responsible for the success of the whole organization.

Does this seem counterintuitive?

If you hold onto the combo view long enough, and let it sink in, you can see that that's exactly how you want everyone, including yourself, to operate. Another example:

The success of this book must largely rest on my shoulders,

since I am its author. Surely the publisher and all of its distribution arms must have some accountability as well. Shall we say it's 85% on my shoulders and 15% on theirs?

That's how businesses usually think.

How about I take 100% and the publisher takes 100% as well? It would certainly avoid a parsing of accountability should it fail. (Or, perhaps I should say it would allow both parties to take full credit when it succeeds!)

It seems to me that if we all had our heads wrapped around full accountability we would get a lot more accomplished. But our egos tend to resist such thinking. Let it go, I say. Go ahead. You touch it; you own it.

FROM DEPENDENCY TO INTRADEPENDENCY

It could be argued that the capacity to transcend the either/or thinking style of egocentricity depends on how mature you are. This makes some sense. But I would argue there is a role for will — and thus for self-esteem, and thus for self-management — as well.

One psychological view is that there are definable stages in a person's development. The first stage, the one we are in at birth, is when we are "dependent." We depend on our caregivers for everything we need. Eventually we discover that we actually are separate from our teddy bears and family members and we start to act that way. We become "independent." This goes on for some time, until we find a mate and we experience "co-dependence." Finally, as we age we begin to realize the interconnectedness of people and things. We are perhaps more sensitive to the environment. We see how an action produces reactions and become more accountable for the impact we have on the world around us. This is "interdependence."

A smart man I know speculates on the possibility of "intradependence." He wonders whether, when we see ourselves about as far from ego as it's possible to get, we are seeing ourselves in some way *as* the universe. I was exposed to another version of this in the work of Roberto Assagioli, the founder of the psychotherapeutic movement known as psychosynthesis. Assagioli's term for this higher perspective is Transpersonal Self, the part of each of us that is connected to the rest of the world.

Getting beyond ego in the way we are exploring would be at least moving from dependency to interdependency. From the self-centric place, the ego place, one is too occupied by the stunning paradox to see the simple reconciliation. But from a "higher" place, a less restricted or narrow perspective — perhaps a more mature perspective that can recognize the interconnectedness of people and things — it all becomes simple.

It's a question of where you put your attention.

Your Turn

Let's talk about you for a moment. Our goal is to see that you can assume the conjoining orientation and address your own ego-centricity.

First of all, you don't have to criticize yourself for anything you've done so far. No, as good polarity seers we get that there are strengths to your style. Your ego is an Is/Ought problem, not an It one. We don't want to negate those strengths.

Perhaps your ego shows up as a kind of sadness where you see yourself as below others or below where you think you should be. The upside to that might be your humility and your willingness to take responsibility. Nope, there's nothing wrong with you. By holding onto that humility and personal accountability, and adding to it a concerted effort to manage the harmful patterns in your self-talk, you can stop seeing yourself as below others. You can see yourself as a capable, willing agent of change. This is actually a matter of choice. Put your attention on the challenges around you as they relate to the mission and implement plans to reach your targets.

Perhaps your ego shows up as someone who sees himself as above others. Maybe people have told you that you are full of yourself. The upside of that is that you have learned to project confidence. Good. The downside is that others mumble to themselves about your self-centeredness. And, in one way or another, you lose them. But you are not that ego. You are actually a facilitator of progress. Allow yourself permission to draw less attention to yourself. Instead, focus on what others are saying. Honor their contribution to the workplace and to the conversation. Be grateful that they are giving you their time. If part of you thinks you're special, spend no time on that part. It's not who you are. Instead, do the job. Connect with others. Leverage their strengths. Don't talk about yourself.

Perhaps your ego shows up as a teeth-gritting machine out to tackle and overcome a monster challenge. It's you versus the monster. Your upside is your will. The downside is that your attack blinds you to possible strategies that only a relaxed perspective can offer. It might also blind you to the needs of others. And that's really not rational of you. They are, after all, the people you need in order to achieve the goal.

Perhaps your ego shows up as threatened by the egos of others. So you wrestle for private control, to maintain your position, to win, to hide. But you are not that threatened entity. You are actually a capable chooser of what to do. Rising above the dynamic created by the threat means letting it go. Eyes on the ball. Don't invest in the game. Catch yourself being hooked and just don't go there. Redirect your attention to the mission. Do things to elevate your own self-esteem — things that perhaps you don't like to do. Do them because you can. And even because you don't want to do them.

But neither you nor I is naïve enough to believe that these are things you can just do. The point of this chapter is that you need to direct your attention differently. Rather than seeing yourself as below, above, or against others, shift your orientation. Embrace both sides of the circumstances that define the polarities you face, recognize the upsides to the things that trouble you, and seek, from that revised vantage point, to nurture healthy relationships, a pervasive sense of ownership, and mutual goal fulfillment into your place of work.

Some of your ability to choose to redirect your attention and to sustain that choice comes from your self-esteem. You can develop your self-esteem, as we discussed in chapter six, by practicing the choice to override impulses. You can also get your boss to read this book so that he or she knows more about the impact of self-esteem on employee engagement. Finally, you can also elevate your capacity to choose your reaction by being more aware of your perspective on things and shifting it.

SHIFTING PERSPECTIVES

In concluding this chapter, let's get specific. Bring to mind a problem or matter that bugs you and choose to adopt the unifying perspective. Here's an example.

Let's say you are sitting scanning your desk to see what's popping up in your world today and a thought crosses your mind:

There's a problem. Melinda often does not double-check her work. She just sent me a draft of an email she wants to distribute and it's not well thought out. I really don't like having to double-check her work.

I see what I guess is the upside to this tendency of hers: it's that she is trying her best to get a lot of things done. And I respect her effort. This book is saying I'm supposed to recognize that as an Is/Ought problem (because I can see the upside) and I'm supposed to direct my attention to the quality of her effort and the realistic goal of her double-checking what she produces. Somehow that's supposed to represent the unifying perspective.

Okay. Go.

Hmm. She is carrying a big load; she is multi-tasking like mad; in her effort to do so, she doesn't stop to double-check.

I need to speak to her — not about this particular instance being problematic for me (because it's not about me and because pattern recognition is more instructive than specific citations of slips) — but about my respect for her effort and my suggestion that when she thinks she's got something off her plate, she should take an extra sixty seconds to review and look for slips.

And now, talk to her.

CHAPTER ELEVEN

DOES IT WORK?

I realize there may still be some doubt in your mind about the practicality of the material in this book. You may have wondered whether the theory actually works in the hardcore business cultures that most of us come from.

I can answer that with an unequivocal yes. It works in my own firm, which has infused into its culture the values espoused in this book. And it works in the organizations of the leaders we have been teaching for over twenty years.

I don't claim that it does so perfectly. We live and work in the real world. We are a group of human beings with our own challenges and struggles. Some days are better than others.

In concluding this book, I want to explore the question, "Does it work?" by letting you hear from several people in my firm. I have asked five of them — all long-time employees — to collect their thoughts on this question. Each of them manages a team.

One of them, Lisa Tomassetti, is our office manager. The other four, along with me, make up the senior leadership of the firm. One of them is Barbara Gaiptman. She is in charge of client relations. That includes the marketing of our services. Another, Sean Verhoeven, is responsible for all "classroom" events; that is, when one of our facilitators conducts some kind of session, he owns it. Suzanne Carlaw leads the project leadership team, making sure that projects go as planned. Last, but not least, is Lynne Gallacher. She is in charge of design and measurement; her team sculpts measurable learning initiatives for clients.

The five of them weigh in on two related and critical leadership paradoxes raised in this book. The first is the Paradox of Influence — that the more focused we are on getting others to do certain things, the less likely it is that we'll get our way. The second is the Paradox of Judgment — that we must be non-judgmental while we judge. These paradoxes are perfect examples of the leader's need to climb out of ego to see things from a higher vantage point. They both call for two orientations to be conjoined: self and other. On the *self* side is our sense that we want what we want and we believe what we believe — egocentricity in its purest form. On the *other* side is our favorable view of the other person, the employee. We need to integrate these things. I have asked for their remarks on the viability of this integration.

As you would predict, my colleagues will say some favorable things about how I have behaved as a leader and in how they behave as leaders of their own teams. But we have our challenges as well. We'll see how they describe them too.

THE PARADOX OF INFLUENCE

The more determined we are to get our way as leaders, the less likely the people we lead are to give it to us. This is because getting our own way with people depends on getting them to listen to us, and when we strongly want our own way, our self-talk deafens us to what they have to say.

The trick is to focus on team members and their self-esteem, rather than ourselves. The result is elevated commitment.

Barbara Gaiptman says that transcending this paradox is an ongoing affair. "I continue to learn about the importance of validating employee self-esteem and about the relationship between self-esteem and the capacity to commit. I see that team members are more able and likely to do their best when the leader takes the time to connect with them. I am sensitive to how my emotions and mood can influence team members and ultimately impact the performance of the team."

Another way of putting this is to say that leaders are at their influential best when they pull rather than push. Lisa Tomassetti initially had a little trouble with the *lack* of push.

"One of the things we're big on in our company is empowerment. Sometimes it can be quite frustrating. There are times when I just want the boss to tell me what to do. It has yet to happen. I always get the same answer: 'What do *you* think we should do?' Yet the beauty of that empowerment philosophy is that he has never judged me when I've made the wrong decision. Not once! And he doesn't dwell on the 'should haves' — we quickly move on. This has a positive, nurturing effect on my spirit. It makes me want to be my best. It evokes a feeling of reciprocity."

Sean Verhoeven echoes this. "I always feel heard and because of this I am more open to fulfill the task, and do so with an elevated sense of self."

Lisa Tomassetti describes high self-esteem's trickle-down effect. "Because I like the way my boss treats me, I'm going to adopt the same style with my reports. It becomes contagious. Soon you have a culture of empowerment and a team of agents. Things get done efficiently and effectively, with no red tape to speak of. I've been part of many projects that seem to flow effortlessly from start to finish, yielding truly satisfying results. Everyone on the team was in sync, with no ego engagement. Decisions were made on the spot, with no second-guessing of each other. Everyone had the same goal in mind. The client was happy and the team was happy."

Suzanne Carlaw says of this: "I believe my time here has allowed me to experience, and to practice, a higher level of leadership. I have experienced from our leadership team a continual demonstration of openness, positive regard, and support for my areas of development. Because this is combined with clarity and consistency of expectations, my sense of agency and accountability is high. Expectations are high, and boy, do I feel accountable!"

THE PARADOX OF JUDGMENT

One of the main roles of leaders is to judge and at the same time be rigorously non-judgmental. How can leaders resolve this paradox? Leaders must learn to restrain their egos while acting as judges. My counsel is to get your ego out of the picture — stick with the facts and watch what comes out of your mouth.

But it can be tempting to fall off the non-judgmental wagon when someone does something wrong. Fortunately, as Suzanne reports, when something goes amiss, "The focus is not on what has been lost, but on providing guidance, and on determining how processes and systems can help support any required shift. Underlying this approach is the unconditional positive regard principle that works with our results-orientation to make the company a wonderful place in which to make a contribution and reach success."

Lisa remembers being at the receiving end of this unstuck paradox.

"I started working at HORN fifteen years ago, right out of university. It was my first real job. Art was scheduled to conduct a training session at a remote resort for a big client. I was responsible for making sure the training manuals arrived at the destination well before the session date. In this particular case I forgot to call the resort ahead of time and, as luck would have it, the manuals had not arrived. He called me the morning of the session and ever so calmly told me that the manuals weren't there. I immediately went into panic mode. You can imagine my self-talk — 'He's going to fire my butt! How's this going to look on my résumé?'

"I spent the entire day trying to track down the box, to no avail. Shortly after the session, he called from his car to say the session went well, sans training materials, and that as he was leaving the resort he saw the courier van pull up (undoubtedly with our manuals inside). I remember sobbing like a baby as he was telling me this.

"What happened next will be forever etched on my brain. Instead of reprimanding me (which I was totally prepared for), he actually started consoling me! I was amazed. Here's a guy who I'm sure had a tough time pulling off a superb session without manuals, and instead of being furious he was actually trying to make *me* feel better. No anger, no judgments. He had already moved on. His attitude had a profound effect on me. It shaped the way I interacted with colleagues from then on. If my manager could forgive and forget, why couldn't I?"

Facing Challenges

No workplace, no matter how closely it hues to the principles of a book such as this, is perfect, and the same goes for the people who work there. So how do these employees describe the challenges they face working within this culture and the challenge we as a team face in keeping these values alive?

Barb starts us off: "Where is our opportunity for development? Because of the effort we make to fully understand and empathize with our colleagues, we sometimes hold back from engaging in candid dialogue and thereby deny ourselves the benefits that contention can bring. And because of our future-orientation, we can miss the opportunity to debrief and learn from past events."

Achieving the right leadership balance is an ongoing challenge. As Sean puts it: "There have indeed been instances where our level of empathy and understanding was so strong that we allowed ourselves or other team members off the hook too easily. Of course when stress levels rise we can be very focused, and perhaps too direct with our communication and expectations of others. Perhaps we even allow people off the hook sometimes, as long as they admit that they had some ownership of undesirable events."

Here's Lynne's take on the topic of stress and workload: "A more selfish adjustment for me is in consistently delivering and doing what it takes to deliver on commitments that our highly client-centric organization makes to its clients. It means a radical mindset shift from 'No, we can't do this' to 'How can we make it work?' At the same time, on occasion, it means being adaptable and flexible to adjusting personal plans to meet short-term client deadlines and at times it's just simply tiring."

Suzanne agrees that "we are not always at the top of our values game individually or collectively. However, goal focus, open disclosure, and agency are the basics day-to-day. The other elements are apparent most of the time; sometimes less so when we are under business pressure.

"We celebrate our achievements. We review as a team the quite rare occasions when we mess up. These reviews are characterized by open disclosure, active listening, empathy, and agency. The goals supporting these reviews are profitability, professional growth, and client-orientation.

"This company is a work-in-progress with purpose and integrity, in my view. We can't claim that we work typically in flow, but we try to practice the values, and we do have many golden flow moments."

MAKING THESE IDEAS WORK FOR YOUR ORGANIZATION

What are the themes in these comments from my pals? That we're okay; and we have a lot of evolving to do. They are both true. We fall off the wagon, forgetting to empathize, sometimes getting overly focused. Sometimes we don't invest in the dialectic of our own conflicting opinions and so we miss opportunities to grow.

On a daily basis, however, we speak the language of this book, hold each other in high regard, and inspire each other to reach results together.

"You will hear the language of this book used regularly at HORN," Suzanne says. "For example, someone will say, 'This was my self-talk as you were telling me this . . .' This common language is incredibly useful in working with each other."

What about you and your team? Can this kind of system work for you? What's it like for someone to adopt this leadership style, or adapt to joining this culture? Again I turn to my group of five, because in one way or another they teach these principles day in and day out to leaders in other organizations.

Suzanne believes the mechanism for achieving the beyond ego culture is "like attracting like." As she puts it: "A beyond ego culture influences an organization's recruiting decisions. As it works in this framework, it gradually builds critical mass from within. This critical mass makes an organization collectively and individually more effective in living out the values and being successful as an organization."

Sean adds that "working in this way creates 'something special in the air.' People from the outside observe a genuine, purely authentic, supportive organization that strives to validate and connect in a humanistic way with all of its internal and external customers. This is what we strive to be: an organization that at the same time craves goal fulfillment and holds everyone accountable to 'be their word' and deliver."

Barb sets out the ideal, which she says is more reachable than usually thought. "Organizations really can develop a culture that is positive, optimistic, collaborative, authentic, and trusting. A culture in which team members seem connected to one another, working in a non-political environment in which there is no sense of individuals trying to sabotage others."

A beyond ego culture is capable of having a relentless focus on clients' needs, according to Lynne. "Leaders and employees have a make-it-happen, result-focused attitude. Little time is spent on unproductive, internal positioning and posturing. These organizations are void of the tiring and frustrating processes of approval. They don't spend a lot of time on corporate reporting and administration. Rather, they have a productive focus on delivering short-term results while building internal capabilities for the future."

Lisa wraps things up on a realistic — and very hopeful — note. "The nice thing is that we all know where we're lacking. I, for example, am very aware of my less than perfect empathy skills. I'm also an enabler, taking care of things rather than empowering my colleagues. However, I consider myself pretty good with commitment and agency. I bet you could ask any one of my colleagues to describe themselves in terms of where they are out of balance in these three things, and they would be bang on.

"However, isn't recognizing your weakness half the battle? Perhaps paradise is within reach after all!"

Suggested Reading

Assagioli, Roberto. *The Act of Will*. Penguin Books, 1974.

Branden, Nathaniel. *The Psychology of Self-Esteem*. Bantam Books, 1969.

Carse, James P. *Breakfast at the Victory*. HarperCollins Canada, 1995.

Csikszentmihalyi, Mihaly. *Flow: The Psychology of Optimal Experience*. Harper Perennial, 1991.

Damasio, Antonio R. *Descartes' Error: Emotion, Reason, and the Human Brain*. Grosset/Putnam, 1994.

Dennett, Daniel C. *Consciousness Explained*. Little, Brown, 1991.

Ellis, Albert and Robert A. Harper. *A New Guide to Rational Living*. Wilshire Book Company, 1975.

Epstein, Mark. *Thoughts Without a Thinker*. Basic Books, 1995.

Ferrucci, Piero. *What We May Be*. J.P. Tarcher, 1982.

Fromm, Erich. *The Art of Loving*. Harper Perennial, 2000.

Goleman, Daniel. *Emotional Intelligence*. Bantam Books, 1995.

Gladwell, Malcolm. *Blink: The Power of Thinking Without Thinking*. Little, Brown, 2005.

Hanh, Thich Nhat. *The Miracle of Mindfulness: An Introduction to the Practice of Meditation*. Beacon, 1999.

Helmstetter, Shad. *What to Say When You Talk to Your Self*. Pocket Books, 1986.

Horn, Art. *Face It: Recognizing and Conquering the Hidden Fear That Drives All Conflict at Work*. Amacom, 2004.

Horn, Art. *Gifts of Leadership: Team Building Through Focus and Empathy*. Stoddart, 1997.

James, William. *The Principles of Psychology, Volume One*. Dover Publications, 1950.

Jaynes, Julian. *The Origin of Consciousness in the Breakdown of the Bicameral Mind*. Houghton Mifflin, 1990.

Jones, Michael. *Artful Leadership: Awakening the Commons of the Imagination*. Trafford, 2007.

Maslow, Abraham H. *Motivation and Personality*, Second Edition. Harper & Row, 1954.

Norretranders, Tor. *The User Illusion*. Penguin USA, 1998.

Ornstein, Robert. *The Roots of the Self*. Harper San Francisco, 1993.

Peck, M. Scott. *The Road Less Traveled and Beyond: Spiritual Growth in an Age of Anxiety*. Simon & Schuster, 1997.

Pert, Candace B. *Molecules of Emotion*. Scribner, 1997.

Rogers, Carl R. *A Way of Being*. Houghton Mifflin, 1980.

Rogers, Carl R. *On Becoming a Person*. Houghton Mifflin, 1961.

Sartre, Jean-Paul. *Being and Nothingness*. Washington Square Press, 1966.

Seligman, Martin E.P. *Learned Optimism: How to Change Your Mind and Your Life*. Pocket Books, 1992.

Wegner, Daniel M. *White Bears and Other Unwanted Thoughts: Suppression, Obsession and the Psychology of Mental Control*. Guilford Publications, 1994.

Wilber, Ken. *A Brief History of Everything*. Shambhala, 1996.

Index